CREATING SAFE SCHOOL ENVIRONMENTS

From Small Steps to Sustainable Change

PETER G. JAFFE

CLAIRE V. CROOKS

C. LYNN WATSON

The Althouse Press

The Althouse Press
Faculty of Education, The University of Western Ontario
Jaffe, Crooks, and Watson, CREATING SAFE SCHOOL ENVIRONMENTS:
FROM SMALL STEPS TO SUSTAINABLE CHANGE

First published in Canada in 2009 by
THE ALTHOUSE PRESS
Dean: *Julia O'Sullivan*
Director of Publications: Greg Dickinson
Faculty of Education, The University of Western Ontario
1137 Western Road, London, Ontario, Canada N6G 1G7

Reprinted: 2010, 2012, 2014

Editorial Assistants: *Katherine Butson, Shanna Burns*
Cover Design: *Louise Gadbois, Brandon Watson*

Library and Archives Canada Cataloguing in Publication

Jaffe, Peter, 1948-
    Creating safe school environments: from small steps to sustainable change / Peter G. Jaffe,
Claire V. Crooks, C. Lynn Watson.

Includes bibliographical references.
ISBN 978-0-920354-70-4

    1. School violence--Prevention. 2. Schools--Safety measures. 3. School management and
organization. I. Crooks, Claire V. II. Watson, C. Lynn, 1943- III. Title.

LB3013.3.J33 2009   371.7'82   C2009-903921-4

TABLE OF CONTENTS

ACKNOWLEDGEMENTS

This book is a culmination of five years work on a project funded by the Ontario Trillium Foundation (OTC). We thank Marilyn Struthers and her team at OTC for having the vision to look beyond funding specific violence prevention programs to investigating the process by which individual programs become sustainable. Throughout our work she has offered invaluable feedback and guidance. Linda Baker, Executive Director of the Centre for Children and Families in the Justice System (CCFJS) has our heartfelt appreciation for her support and encouragement throughout the project. We thank Karen Rhiger of the CCFJS for her capable financial and administrative oversight.

The project upon which this book is based required a great deal of trust and openness from the four school boards that were involved. These boards included the Limestone School Board, Thames Valley District School Board, Toronto District School Board and Rainbow District School Board. We thank the administrators, staff, parents and students from these boards who shared their successes, challenges, and growing pains with great honesty.

We thank the other members of our research team, including Linda Crossley-Hauch, Steve Killip, Ray Hughes, and Jennine Rawana. Collectively they brought great expertise throughout the project, and provided multiple perspectives as researchers, clinicians, educators and administrators. This book represents countless hours of spirited debate and competing perspectives on the meaning of our data and school visits. Each of our team members provided a careful review of an earlier version of this manuscript.

Our project was guided by a committed Provincial Advisory Committee that reflected the broad partnerships required for maintaining safe school environments. We thank the members of this committee and the associations they represented at the time of their involvement including Doug Acton, Ontario Principals' Council; Bob Borden, Ontario School Boards Association; Barb Burkett, Elementary Teachers Federation; Lori Foote, Ontario Secondary School Teachers Federation; Brenda Hopkins, Thames Valley District School Council; Cheryl Nicholls-Jones, Ontario Secondary School Teachers Federation; Darryl Pinnell, Ontario Association of Chiefs of Police; Gerry Treble, Ontario Ministry of Education and Training; Cynthia Lemon, Elementary Teachers' Federation of Ontario; and Graham Pollett, Association of Local Public Health Agencies.

We thank our colleagues who reviewed earlier versions of this book, including Debbie Chiodo, Chris Dennett, Wendy Josephson, and David Tomlin. We thank Debra Pepler for reviewing the book and preparing the Foreword.

We extend our heartfelt thanks and gratitude to our colleague, Shanna Burns, for her tireless efforts and incredible talents in editing and creating a well-presented manuscript. Thanks are also owed to Katherine Butson and Greg Dickinson of The Althouse Press for their thoughtful feedback and assistance and the review provided by their anonymous panel.

Peter Jaffe, Claire Crooks, and Lynn Watson

Imagine a school where every student, staff member, and community visitor felt safe! This is a vision that we hold high for our schools, especially with the growing recognition that positive relationships at school are critical for effective learning. Yet, there is a substantial gap between our vision and the reality in schools today. With our vision and demands for safer schools, we are asking schools to be at the forefront of social-cultural change. We are expecting them to be models of healthy relationships when there are so many models of unhealthy relationships in the families, communities, media, and socio-political contexts where children and youth grow up. Bringing about this social change is complex and challenging; and, to date, there has been little coherence in the pathways and signposts to guide schools in their safe schools efforts.

In this book on creating safe school environments, Jaffe, Crooks, and Watson have finally provided the comprehensive and practical guides needed for a coordinated and sustained effort to ensure our schools are safe so that all children can learn. Their book is primarily written for principals who provide vital leadership in guiding school communities through the ongoing processes of establishing a vision, policies, and procedures that sustain a positive school climate and prevent bullying and violence. Research on bullying prevention in schools has repeatedly shown that principals' leadership is essential to establishing a foundation of collaboration across all groups within the school community—staff, students, parents, and community partners. The stages of change model that Jaffe, Crooks, and Watson have adapted for this journey to sustaining safe schools provides principals with tools to recognize where their schools are in the change process and with tools to make the appropriate change. Their Safe Schools Continuum model comprises three stages: developing awareness, planning and responding, and educating and leading. They provide excellent illustrations of elementary and secondary schools at different stages on the Safe Schools Continuum.

What do principals need to achieve a positive school climate? It is no longer sufficient to focus on markers of academic achievement in evaluating the effectiveness of schools. We now recognize that all relationships in schools matter: those among staff, among students, and between staff and students. PREVNet—the Promoting Relationships and Eliminating Violence Network has identified four strategy pillars to bring about social-cultural change in Canada. These apply well to principals' efforts to bring about social change by leading their school communities in education and training, assessment and evaluation, prevention and intervention, and in establishing policies and procedures that ensure positive social interactions. In this book, Jaffe, Crooks, and Watson provide critical insights for all four of these foundations for social change:

- The book is based on years of research on evidence-based violence prevention programs in schools, the ASAP program, and the Fourth R program. The authors recommend starting by educating the Safe Schools Committee, which in turn can build awareness and understanding throughout the school.
- After establishing an understanding of safe school topics such as bullying and harassment, the authors recommend assessing schools' needs through a variety of methods including surveys of students, staff and parents, focus groups, audits of the physical plant, and a review of existing programs and policies. They point readers to evidence-based and available assessment tools.
- Based on the assessment of the safety of relationships within their schools, principals and their Safe Schools Committees can choose where to start in preventing and intervening to ensure a safe school. There are questions and guidelines linked to each of the three stages of change to guide principals and committees in reviewing their own policies, procedures, and interventions, as well as suggestions for evaluating the suitability of packaged programs.

- To improve and sustain efforts to promote safe schools, it is essential to review and renew the policies and procedures relating to all aspects of school safety. Again, Jaffe and his colleagues illustrate how principals can lead their schools through a consideration of policies and procedures, at a stage of change that fits with the school's current standing on the Safe Schools Continuum.

With this book, Jaffe, Crooks, and Watson have provided critical tools for principals to understand their schools' needs by considering where they are on the change spectrum and then to effectively promote safe schools by matching strategies and programs to the school's stage of change. The authors provide support for principals to lead their schools through stages of awareness, planning, and implementation to a sustainable and enriching safe school context. In this book, Jaffe, Crooks, and Watson have gathered information on all of these foundational building blocks for change. The tools for change are now readily available to those who need them—school principals, safe schools committees, and all those within a school community who are committed to working collaboratively to create positive, inclusive relationships and a positive climate in their schools. I extend my deep appreciation to the authors for this significant contribution to our collective efforts to promote safe and healthy schools and to bring about social-cultural change in the broader society.

Debra J. Pepler, Ph.D., C.Psych.
Distinguished Research Professor of Psychology, York University
Senior Associate Scientist, The Hospital for Sick Children
Scientific Co-Director, Promoting Relationships and Eliminating Violence Network

PETER JAFFE, PH.D., C.PSYCH.

Dr. Jaffe is Academic Director of the Centre for Research & Education on Violence Against Women and Children and a Professor at The Faculty of Education, The University of Western Ontario. He is also the Founding Director for the Centre for Children and Families in the Justice System of the London Family Court Clinic (CCFJS; 1975-2001) and continues to act as a consultant to the CCFJS, which is a children's mental health centre specializing on issues which bring children and families into the justice system. He is an Adjunct Professor to the departments of Psychology and Psychiatry at the University of Western Ontario. He has co-authored eight books, 24 chapters, and over 75 articles related to children, families, and the justice system. He has presented workshops across Canada and the United States, as well as Australia, New Zealand and Europe, to various groups including educators, judges, lawyers, and mental health professionals. Dr. Jaffe has been a trustee for the London Board of Education (now the Thames Valley District School Board) since 1980, and he has served two terms as Chairperson.

CLAIRE CROOKS, PH.D., C.PSYCH.

Dr. Crooks is the Associate Director of the CAMH Centre for Prevention Science in London, Ontario and an Adjunct Professor at The University of Western Ontario (Education; Health Sciences; and Psychology departments). Her main research interests include the development and evaluation of school-based violence prevention programming, with a particular emphasis on strengths-based programming for Aboriginal youth. She is co-author of more than 40 articles, chapters, and books on topics including school-based programming with Aboriginal youth, children's exposure to domestic violence, child custody and access, adolescent dating violence and risk behaviour, and trauma. She is co-author of the book, *Adolescent Risk Behaviors: Why teens experiment and strategies to keep them safe* (2006; Wolfe, Jaffe, & Crooks, Yale University Press). She received her undergraduate training from Princeton University in New Jersey, and her M.A. and Ph.D. from Queen's University.

LYNN WATSON, M.ED.

Lynn Watson graduated from the University of Western Ontario with a B.A in geography and M.Ed. in Educational Psychology. A former secondary school geography teacher, Lynn has worked as a research assistant on a wide variety of projects. She was involved with the Centre for Children and Families in the Justice System in developing violence prevention programs for schools that resulted in the publishing of A.S.A.P., A School-Based Anti-Violence Program, 1996. She has also prepared an evaluation of an adult learning program with computers for Human Resources Development Canada. Following that project, Lynn took a sabbatical from program evaluation to work as the manager of a busy constituency office for a provincial cabinet minister. Lynn coordinated the Sustainable Strategies for Safe Schools project described in this book.

PROJECT TEAM

LINDA CROSSLEY-HAUCH, M.ED.

Linda Crossley-Hauch is a retired educator with 34 years experience. For 13 years Linda was a secondary school administrator and in her last four years with the board she held the position of Learning Supervisor. Linda has been an active member of several professional organizations, most recently the Thames Valley Secondary School Administrators Council which she chaired in 1999 and which she represented for three years as a member of the Ontario Principals' Council. Throughout her career, Linda has been actively engaged in developing and implementing safe schools initiatives locally, provincially and nationally. She was a member of the Ministry of Education's Advisory Committee on Discipline and the local school board's Safe School Committee, which she chaired for 5 years.

RAY HUGHES, M.ED.

Ray Hughes is a graduate of the University of Toronto (B.P.H.E.). Ray obtained his B.Ed. and M.Ed. from The Faculty of Education, The University of Western Ontario. He has 29 years of experience in education as a teacher, Department Head, and Consultant. He is currently the National Education Coordinator for the Fourth R Project with the University of Western Ontario and an instructor in Safe Schools at The Faculty of Education, The University of Western Ontario. Ray coordinates the implementation of the Fourth R Project across Canada through partnerships with Alliance partners and school boards. He is a member of the Ontario Safe Schools Action Team. The mandate of the Action Team is to draw on best practices from across Ontario and to advise the Minister of Education on all aspects of school safety.

STEVE KILLIP, PH.D.

Steve Killip received his PhD in Psychology from the University of Calgary. Since 1989 he has been the Manager, Research, Assessment and Accountability of the Research and Assessment Department at the Thames Valley District School Board. With a focus on corporate data management and analysis, student assessment, and research and evaluation studies the department serves the needs of students, staff and community through evidence informed practice and leadership.

JENNINE RAWANA, PH.D., C.PSYCH.

Dr. Rawana is currently an Assistant Professor in the Psychology Department at York University. She completed her Ph.D. in Clinical Psychology at Lakehead University and her clinical internship in the Child, Youth and Family Program with the Centre for Addiction and Mental Health (CAMH) in Toronto. Dr. Rawana has research interests in adolescent mental health including preventing risky behaviours and seasonal variations in mood (in both adults and adolescents). She has worked with schools in a variety of capacities including assessment, research, and consultation.

CENTRE FOR RESEARCH AND EDUCATION ON VIOLENCE AGAINST WOMEN AND CHILDREN

The Centre promotes the development of community-centred, action research on violence against women and children. The Centre's role is to facilitate the cooperation of individuals, groups and institutions representing the diversity of the community to pursue research questions and training opportunities to understand and prevent abuse. It serves local, national and international communities by producing useful information and tools to assist in the daily work against violence toward women and children. Researchers at the Centre have developed numerous resources for educators, including lesson plans related to media violence for every grade, and learning resources on gender equity and youth engagement strategies. Many of these resources are available for free download on the website.

www.crvawc.ca

CAMH CENTRE FOR PREVENTION SCIENCE

The CAMH Centre for Prevention Science is the home of *Strategies for Healthy Youth Relationships,* a consortium of researchers and professionals dedicated to promoting healthy adolescent relationships and reducing risk behaviours. Members of the Centre develop and evaluate programs, resources and training materials for educators and other front-line professionals who work with youth. Fourth R initiatives use best practice approaches to target multiple forms of violence, including bullying, dating violence, peer violence, and group violence. By building healthy school environments we provide opportunities to engage students in developing healthy relationships and decision-making to provide a solid foundation for their learning experience. Increasing youth relationship skills and targeting risk behaviour with a harm reduction approach empowers adolescents to make healthier decisions about relationships, substance use and sexual behaviour. There are some resources available for download on the website (including a toolkit for engaging and empowering Aboriginal youth) and others that can be ordered.

www.youthrelationships.org

CENTRE FOR CHILDREN AND FAMILIES IN THE JUSTICE SYSTEM

The Centre for Children and Families in the Justice System (formerly the London Family Court Clinic) is a non-profit social service agency helping children and families involved with the justice system as victims of crime, witnesses of crime, parties in custody disputes, subjects of child protection proceedings, litigants in civil suits for compensation, teenagers in therapeutic care settings, or youthful offenders. The Centre is known around the world for their grounded approach to understanding children exposed to domestic violence, supporting their mothers, and creating training resources for service deliverers. The Centre for Children and Families in the Justice System has numerous resources available, including handbooks for various educators as well as social service and justice professionals on supporting children exposed to domestic violence, and victims of woman abuse.

www.lfcc.on.ca

This book was written to provide school communities with a systematic framework for assessing school safety needs and developing a plan to address those needs in a sustainable manner. Specifically, we have written this book to speak to administrators, who are the heads of all safe schools initiatives. This book will also be a valuable resource to other safe school leaders, whether they are educators, community partners, or parents who are contributing to safe school initiatives at the school or system level. It is our hope that this book will provide you and your whole school community with valuable and practical tools. As authors we brought together the collective wisdom of our diverse experiences in roles as teachers, administrators, trustees, researchers and psychologists. Many of these ideas emerged from our collaborative research with educators, parents and students in 23 schools across Ontario. We were motivated to share the lessons we learned with other school administrators and educators who are facing the same thorny issues. First and foremost in our lessons is that there are no quick fixes. Violence prevention is not an event. Violence prevention has to be an ongoing and sustainable process.

The safety of schools was rarely a topic of conversation in past generations. Now, hardly a week goes by without a media account of an incident of school violence. In recent years, tragic events in schools have made every parent, teacher, and student more aware of the potential for violence in schools and the need to be more vigilant about school safety. Just mentioning a particular city or school name can make us reflect on a horrific tragedy. Columbine in the United States and W.R. Myers in Taber, Alberta and Toronto's C.W. Jeffreys Collegiate Institute each represent a call for action. While violence of this magnitude is relatively rare, these incidents serve to focus media and public attention on the issue of school safety. These school shootings are the tip of an enormous iceberg made up of the bullying, harassment, racism, and sexism that surrounds our children.

The Columbine incident, in particular, led to a widespread feeling of "if it can happen there it can happen anywhere." As the ensuing inquest revealed, Columbine High School is an upper-middle class suburban school with high scholastic standards.[1] It is well known for the success of its athletic teams, and a large majority of its graduates go on to university. Like many other schools shootings, the Columbine tragedy was perpetrated by students who had been bullied at school and who were seeking to kill familiar students and teachers. This tragedy also highlighted the fact that young people are more likely to experience violence at the hands of somebody they know. In fact, contrary to common fears of the unknown assailant, most school violence is embedded in established peer and dating relationships.

Columbine is the most recognizable incident on the basis of sheer number of casualties (13 killed and 23 severely injured), but it is certainly not the only tragedy of this type. At W.R. Myers High School in Taber, Alberta, one week after the shooting at Columbine, a fourteen-year-old boy entered the school and opened fire with a .22 calibre rifle. He killed young Jason Lang and injured another student. Students reported that the student who perpetrated the crime was unpopular at school and was subject to teasing and name-calling. His mother reported that he was incessantly bullied and was subject to depression.

Across the continent, politicians responded to these shootings with new legislation, policies and procedures designed to ensure school safety. In Ontario, they responded to increased violent incidents in schools with the strict *Safe Schools Act* that emphasized "zero tolerance" for violence and clear and consistent sanctions for students who were perpetrators. More recently, the government established a Safe Schools Action Team[2] to review the *Safe Schools* Act and make recommendations for programs and policies. As of 2009, the Safe Schools Action Team has produced three reports designed to guide safe schools practice in Ontario. The first two reports addressed bullying and made specific recommendations for programming and

---

[1] The Columbine inquest provides a thorough analysis of contributing factors and missed opportunities implicated in the tragedy. The final report, entitled The Report of Governor Bill Owens' Columbine Review Commission, is available at http://www.state.co.us/columbine/Columbine_20Report_WEB.pdf

[2] Called together by the Minister of Education in December, 2004; the Safe School Task Force, its chairperson, Ms. Liz Sandals, and members, Mr. Stu Auty, Dr. Inez Elliston, Mr. Ray Hughes, Dr. Debra Pepler, and Ms. Lynn Ziraldo were charged with reviewing the Safe Schools Act and related policies and programs. The Task Force produced three reports, *Shaping safer schools: A bullying prevention action plan* (November, 2005), Safe schools policy and practice: An agenda for action (June, 2006), and, Shaping a culture of respect in our schools: Promoting safe and healthy relationships (December, 2008).

action plans. As part of these reports, the Task Force recommended programs that promote healthy relationships and conflict resolution for all students. The third report specifically addressed homophobia, sexual harassment and gender-based violence, raising the visibility of problems that have sometimes been swept under the rug. It offered 75 specific recommendations for addressing these types of violence. Addressing school violence was no longer an optional practice. School districts received directives that indicated they were "required to develop and implement policies on bullying prevention and intervention" and given clear deadlines for action. The Safe Schools Task Force also emphasized that the approach to safe schools must include the participation of all parts of society, including schools, community groups, students, and parents. The team's recommendations resulted in new legislation, Bill 212, an *Act to Amend the Education Act in Respect of Behaviour, Discipline and Safety*, which was passed into law in 2007. While sanctions and discipline continue to be one part of the recommended responses, a more balanced approach was recommended, including special programs for students returning from a suspension of more than three days.

Other policy and funding initiatives of the Ontario government, as well as those of governments across Canada and the United States, indicate that violence in schools is still at the top of the education agenda. A number of approaches have been recommended to ensure safe schools. These include school-wide campaigns, celebrations of achievements for the school, groups, or individuals, and day-to-day interaction with students and staff. School councils, safe school teams, parents, students, teachers, staff, administrators, and the community all should be involved in establishing these strategies and approaches to ensure positive school climates and safe schools for learning.

SCHOOL SYSTEM RESPONSE TO VIOLENCE INCIDENTS

Recognizing the need for developing healthy relationships among students and ensuring their connectedness to the wider community is an important first step in preventing violence. In this context of changing legislation and heightened awareness, many schools have increased their emphasis on violence prevention and student safety. However, even the most forward-looking school jurisdictions can be caught off guard when a violent incident occurs in one of their schools. These incidents are the ultimate test for a school district response. The following two examples show how such tragedies can be used to mobilize schools and communities to take a closer look at safe schools.

THAMES VALLEY DISTRICT SCHOOL BOARD

Over the years, the Thames Valley District School Board (TVDSB) has prided itself for being a leader in violence prevention programming. The TVDSB has over 75,000 students in over 180 schools spread across 7,000 square kilometres of urban and rural South-Western Ontario. It was one of the first school boards in Ontario to appoint a Violence Prevention Coordinator to its program department over a decade ago. Nevertheless, on November 26, 2004, the TVDSB was rocked when one of its high school students, Josh Melo, committed suicide. Josh had been the victim of ongoing cyber-bullying by other students. From that one incident, the school system moved from crisis to a thorough analysis of the system to determine what went wrong and, more importantly, how to move forward to prevent bullying within its schools. While the response to Josh's suicide was immediate, it was not impulsive. Even though such a tragedy could well trigger a defensive response, such as denial and silence, the response was well thought out and inclusive. The TVDSB was under great pressure from parents and the media to take immediate action, but they stepped back and made a careful plan that would involve the whole school system in the response.

In December 2004, the TVDSB established a committee to review the environment of safety in their schools. The committee was mandated to investigate two factors. First, the committee was charged with determining why youth do not report experiencing or witnessing bullying and harassment. Second, the committee was to examine what school communities can do to create a culture that encourages youth to report information regarding bullying and harassment.

The committee's work included surveying all students from grades 4 through 12 in the widely spread and populous school district.[3] School level / survey results were communicated

---

[3] The Committee to Review the Environment of Safety in our Schools, Secondary Report, Spring, 2005, and Elementary Report, Spring, 2006; available at http://www.tvdsb.on.ca/safeschools

back to each school along with comparative board-wide results. As part of the process, each school was required to conduct a focus group to review the results of the survey. School administrators then sent their school summaries back to the systems committee, which used the information to develop and implement a system-wide plan for action. The work is ongoing at the school and district level. In 2008 and 2009 the survey, with minor additions, was re-administered to monitor changes related to these initiatives.

TORONTO DISTRICT SCHOOL BOARD

The Toronto District School Board (TDSB) experienced an equally shocking incident in 2007 when 15-year-old Jordan Manners was shot inside the school at C.W. Jeffreys Collegiate Institute in Toronto. Similar to the aftermath of the tragedies in Columbine and Taber, this incident jolted all who thought that schools were safe places. The family and the media demanded answers to how this tragedy could take place and what remedies could be put in place to prevent any future incidents. The TDSB responded in a comprehensive fashion to the calls for an inquiry into this tragic shooting by appointing lawyer Julian Falconer to chair the Community Safety Advisory Panel. The committee's mandate was to review the circumstances surrounding Jordan's shooting and to make recommendations to the school board to ensure that Toronto schools are safe and welcoming environments. However, the TDSB did not wait for the final report to implement a revised policy across the system (see text box). After the release of the report, the TDSB announced a 4 million dollar plan to address school safety involving hiring specialized staff to counsel marginalized youth and professional development on racism and equity issues. The plan gained wide public support. In the words of an editorial in one of the most widely circulated newspapers in Canada, the plan was seen to encompass "sensible measures to curb the physical and sexual violence, bullying and intimidation that turned some Toronto schools into war zones."[4] Full information on the panel report and subsequent response can be found at the TDSB web-site at www.tdsb.on.ca. Almost a year after the report was released Falconer spoke out again declaring that there had been no substantive changes to make schools safer. However, headlines may not capture the significant work going on behind

---

[4] Toronto Star, May 21, 2008, p.8.

the scenes. The Leadership Action Team Report released in May 2008 indicates some of the changes already underway, as well as short- and medium-term goals. Clearly a good blueprint (such as the report provided by Falconer) is an essential step in closing the gap between ideals and reality of schools. Implementing the recommendations of such a report in a complex environment requires much attention and work.[5]

TDSB Revised Policy

- All schools must continue to have a Safe Schools Accountability Framework that includes implementing specific policies, procedures, and programs. These include: mandatory practice of lockdown and fire drills and other safety procedures; and development of Safe School Action Plans and Bullying Prevention Plans. The Superintendents of Education were charged with monitoring compliance across the board.
- All secondary schools must participate in the Empowered Student Partnerships (ESP) program co-sponsored by the Toronto Police Service and the Canadian Safe Schools Network.
- All schools with grades 7 and 9 students must participate in PEACE (Public Education and Crime Eradication), a project developed with the Toronto Police Service. This program will promote awareness of gun and gang violence.
- All TDSB schools must establish a Safe Schools Committee with members representing parents, staff, and community partners. This committee will assist with the development of the Safe Schools Action Plan, including bullying prevention.
- Safe and Caring Schools Weeks must highlight and recognize students and partners who have contributed to developing and sustaining safe and caring schools.

UNDERSTANDING THE SCHOOL SHOOTINGS AS PART OF A LARGER PROBLEM

School shootings make national headlines but reflect only a small and tragic part of an enormous problem. Fundamentally, students need a safe environment in which to learn and succeed. Violence prevention strategies and programs need to focus on healthy lifestyles and relationships, student leadership, empathy, citizenship development, conflict resolution, restorative practice, bullying prevention, and peer mediation. Beyond the tragedies, the major impetus for change in schools has come from movements that view educators as having a central role in promoting social justice in our communities through addressing homophobia, gender violence and sexual harassment. As well, researchers have focused on the negative

---

5 Toronto District School Board (2008). *On the road to health: Leadership Action Team Report. Safe, Caring and Inclusive Schools*. Retrieved June 15 2009
http://www.tdsb.on.ca/wwwdocuments/about_us/media_room/docs/tdsb_lat_report-on_the_road_to_health_200508.pdf

interactions among children and identified bullying as a central form of violence. Awareness of these two issues – both the culture of violence and discrimination as well as problematic individual interactions among children – have increased greatly in the past twenty years.

HOW COMMON ARE BULLYING AND SEXUAL HARASSMENT?

Bullying is a pervasive experience for Canadian children[6] in its many forms. Given the pre-eminence of bullying in the safe schools field, it is important to define the nature and scope of the problem. When we use the term bullying we refer to a form of aggression in which there is an imbalance of power between the bully and the victim. The bully's power can come from real or perceived differences in economic status, social status, religion, ethnicity, disability, age, size, need for special education, sexual orientation, family circumstances, gender, and race. In addition to power imbalance, other key elements include the bully's intent to harm, victim's distress and repeated incidents over time. In social bullying, bullies exclude others from a group or spread gossip or rumours about them. Electronic bullying (also known as cyber bullying), includes spreading rumours and hurtful comments through the use of email, cell phones, and text messaging.

In a survey of Canadian youth in grades 6 to 10, 25% of boys and 21% of girls reported being victims of bullying. Between 2% and 8% reported being victimized regularly (once a week or more). Those who reported perpetrating the bullying behaviours were approximately 25% of boys and 18% of girls. For boys, the behaviour peaked in grade 10, while for girls in grades 7 and 8. Again, a small minority of students (2% to 8%) engaged in this form of aggressive behaviour on a regular basis. A substantive number of these students reported that they behaved as both bullies and victims. According to earlier research, peers are present in 85% of the bullying episodes on the playground and in the school. When the bystanders are factored in to the equation, you can see that the bully's actions affect the majority of students.

---

[6] For more information on bullying and prevalence rates see the Canadian Public Health Association Safe School Study at: http://acsp.cpha.ca/antibullying/english/backinfo/safe_school_study_final.pdf

The importance of having safe schools is supported by the pervasiveness and negative impacts associated with bullying. Students who experience bullying can be affected in a short- and /or long-term manner. For some it is the relatively short-lived embarrassment and discomfort of the actual incident; for others the long-term consequences may include anxiety, depression, social isolation, or even thoughts of suicide. In severe cases bullying can result in post-traumatic stress disorder or suicide attempts. While those who are being bullied at school may be severely affected, the student who exhibits bullying behaviour is also at risk to continue a trajectory of acting out. These students are most likely to become involved in delinquency and substance abuse, sexual harassment, dating violence, and adult criminality. Bystanders are not immune to the impact of the bullying either. All youth and adults exposed to the negative interactions of students may have their well-being and capacity for learning diminished.

Harassment, as a form of gender-based violence includes verbal, psychological, physical and economic abuse that is based on an individual's gender and is intended to control, humiliate or harm that individual. This form of violence is generally directed by boys and men against girls and women and is based on attitude or prejudice, conscious or unconscious, individual or institutional that subordinates an individual or a group of people based on sex and gender identity.[7]

Over 10 years ago the Ontario Secondary School Teachers' Federation funded a study entitled, *The Joke's Over–Student to Student Sexual Harassment in Secondary Schools*.[8] The study found that over 80% of female students reported that they had been sexually harassed in a school setting. This high prevalence rate stems from the measurement approach in that researchers were looking at lifetime prevalence of any single incident of harassment. The researchers discovered that the majority of male students surveyed seemed to take the topic

---

[7] Jaffe, P. & Hughes, R. (2008). Preventing violence against girls: Challenges and opportunities for educators. *Education Forum* Vol. 34, Issue 3, Fall, 2008. For more information see Ontario Ministry of Education and Training (2008). *Shaping a culture of respect in our schools: Promoting safe and healthy relationships.* Available at http://www.edu.gov.on.ca/eng/teachers/RespectCulture.pdf

[8] *The joke's over: Student to student sexual harassment in secondary schools* (1995). A project team from OSSTF/FEESO, the Ontario Women's Directorate, the Violence Prevention Secretariat and the Ministry of Education and Training. This resource includes materials to assist teachers to understand sexual harassment and to develop strategies to eliminate it.

much less seriously than female students, particularly when speaking of being harassed by a female. The study was one of the first to suggest that sexual harassment was a major problem in the Ontario schools and had to be understood as part of a continuum of school violence.

A recent major survey on adolescent risk behaviours in 23 secondary schools found that almost half of the students (43%) reported experiencing sexual harassment in grade 9.[9] Although the rates were similar for girls and boys, the types of harassment experiences differed. The girls were more likely than boys to experience being the recipient of sexual jokes, comments, and unwanted touch, while boys were more likely to be subjected to slurs about homosexuality. Sexual harassment was associated with a range of negative outcomes for girls that included suicidal thoughts, self harm, maladaptive dieting, early dating, substance use, and poor grades. The impact of sexual harassment victimization persisted from grade 9 to grade 11 and was associated with higher risk for other forms of relationship violence at grade 11. Sexual harassment in grade 9 contributed to risk for both internalizing and externalizing problems 2.5 years later. Boys experienced many of the same consequences when harassed but at a lesser frequency and severity. Girls tend to be harassed because they are girls and the boys are most likely to be harassed because they don't conform to perceptions of the ideal masculinity (are perceived as being too feminine or perceived to be gay).

In addition to understanding bullying and harassment in general, it is important to consider other social dynamics that intersect with these behaviours. Racism and other forms of discrimination need to be addressed both as forms of bullying and harassment, but also at a larger systemic level. For example, it is one thing to recognize that Aboriginal youth as a group demonstrate higher rates of behaviour problems such as violence. It is another thing altogether to have an understanding of the historical and current contexts within which those behaviours

---

[9] Chiodo, D., Wolfe, D.A., Crooks, C., Hughes, R., & Jaffe, P. (in press). The impact of sexual harassment victimization by peers on subsequent adolescent victimization and adjustment: A longitudinal study. *Journal of Adolescent Health.*

have developed. It is only through understanding this context that appropriate strategies can be developed and put in place to more effectively engage Aboriginal youth and their families.[10]

THE UNRECOGNIZED FACES OF VIOLENCE

Violence also affects teachers. Teachers' primary concern may be for their students' welfare, but they also need to feel safe and secure at school. In Ontario, three teacher federations (the Elementary Teachers' Federation of Ontario, the Ontario Secondary School Teachers' Federation, and the Ontario English Catholic Teachers' Association) were concerned enough to retain a research company to conduct a survey to obtain information concerning bullying of teaching staff.[11] In total, 1,217 members of the three federations were interviewed over the telephone. They reported that bullying of teachers by students is more prevalent than any other form of bullying (teacher or parent bullying), and that just under four of every 10 teachers in Ontario reported that they have been bullied by their students. Some of the reported incidents included the following: verbal abuse, disrupting classrooms, disrespect, repeated racial, sexual, or religious slurs, repeated attempts at intimidation, vandalizing personal property or belongings, and threats. Based on various reports, it appears that some teachers experience bullying in ways similar to their students. Clearly, many teachers are threatened and harassed within their working environment and do not feel safe. As with all forms of bullying, technological advances, such as social-networking platforms and internet capabilities have increased the avenues through which teachers may experience bullying and harassment.

When dealing with violence faced by children and youth in school, a comprehensive approach must recognize that many youth are exposed to violence in their families. In an average classroom, there might be 3 to 5 children dealing with the aftermath of being abused or

---

[10] Crooks, C.V., Chiodo, D., & Thomas, T. (2009). *Engaging and empowering Aboriginal youth: A toolkit for service providers.* Victoria, BC: Trafford Press.

[11] Matsui, J. & Lang Research. (2005). *Bullying in the workplace: A survey of Ontario's elementary and secondary school teachers and educational workers.* For ETFO, OECTA & OSSTF. Available online at http://www.oecta.on.ca/pdfs/bullying_execsum.pdf

exposed to violence in their own home.[12] Domestic violence is one of the most common forms of violence that children witness. Some efforts have been directed at educators to recognize their potential role and responsibility in responding to children exposed to domestic violence (see www.lfcc.on.ca for an educator's handbook on this issue). The role of school-based programming in preventing violence and promoting healthy relationships has even been recognized by the Office of the Chief Coroner in Ontario as a potential factor in preventing domestic homicides.

Discussion of violence opens the door to a broader definition of forms of abuse in different contexts. Some students may have to cope with the aftermath of sexual abuse in the context of family and/or trust relationships with professionals involved in their care. Discussions of abuse and harassment in school have to include the fact that the perpetrator may be a teacher or other trusted adult. This topic is a sensitive one to address with students since it is more comfortable to discuss "stranger danger" rather than abuse by individuals like teachers who have such a significant and meaningful role in their lives. There is still much resistance to examining the abusive behaviour of a small number of educators. Recognizing that adults working in schools can and do injure the youth they are expected to protect is painful for educators and the public to address.[13] The recent public inquiry into historical child abuse by adults in a variety of community institutions highlighted the need for schools to play a critical role in early identification and prevention programs in this area.[14] Although this topic is beyond the scope of this book, we encourage the reader to explore these important references.

---

[12] Sudermann, M., Jaffe, P.G., & Schieck, E. (1996). *Bullying: Information for parents and teachers*. London, ON: London Family Court Clinic. Available online at http://www.lfcc.on.ca/bully.htm

[13] For a thorough analysis of the dynamics which make it difficult to address teachers who perpetrate violence and abuse, see the report arising from the Robins Review. Robins, S. L. (2000). *Protecting our students: A review to identify and prevent sexual misconduct in Ontario schools*. Toronto, ON: Queen's Printer.

[14] For a discussion of these issues please see the evidence gathered by the Cornwall Public Inquiry as well as the final report and recommendations at http://www.cornwallinquiry.ca/en/. The Cornwall Public Inquiry was established by the Government of Ontario on April 14, 2005, under the Public Inquiries Act. The mandate of the Commission is to inquire into and report on the events surrounding allegations of abuse of young people in Cornwall by examining the response of the justice system and other public institutions to the allegations.

There are numerous organizations and researchers across Canada dedicated to the prevention of violence for youth. Recently, many of these organizations aligned to create PREVNet[15] (Promoting Relationships and Eliminating Violence Network)—the first national strategy to eliminate violence for all children and to promote the formation of healthy relationships. PREVNet includes Canada's leading researchers, national organizations, governments, and communities, under the leadership of Dr. Debra Pepler at York University and Dr. Wendy Craig at Queen's University. The partnership is attempting to standardize approaches and increase communication among researchers and policy makers and those who work on the front line. The vision is for all adults who work with youth to have a similar level of understanding about the root causes of bullying and effective strategies for prevention, regardless of whether that adult is a swim coach on Vancouver Island, a scout leader in Estevan, or a dance teacher in Corner Brook. Among the member organizations of PREVNet are educational partners such as the Canadian Association of Principals, the Canadian Teacher's Federation, and the Canadian School Boards Association, as well as organizations as diverse as the Canadian Safety Council, Kids' Help Phone, and the Family Channel. This vision is being realized through attempts to standardize messages among researchers (to avoid people being overloaded with seemingly contradictory information) and to share leading research in meaningful ways. For example, extensive work has been done between PREVNet researchers and Girl Guides of Canada to develop suitable violence prevention programs and strategies. PREVnet seeks to work with all front line workers in the community, including teachers. Through working with organizations that have a national scope, dissemination of effective strategies far surpasses that achieved by any one local effort.

As the activities of these educators, researchers, and community agencies indicate, awareness of violence in schools during the past decade has gone from being an afterthought to being a key component of educational thought and planning. The safe schools agenda has become a legitimate and massive force of its own, and the vast majority of educators are aware

---

[15] More information is available on the PREVNet website at www.prevnet.ca.

that providing a safe, caring environment is a critical component of educating children today. First and foremost, there are no quick fixes. Violence prevention is not an event. Violence prevention has to be an ongoing and sustainable process

The good news is that now the role of schools in preventing bullying is no longer debated; indeed, many educators want to be leaders in the effort against violence. The bad news is that some people are still looking for quick solutions; find the bullies and violent kids and suspend or expel them, and have more physical security and monitoring. In addition, many people, including those in the media, continue to emphasize extreme and stranger-perpetrated violence, rather than the daily reality of bullying, harassment, and abuse that occurs in schools.

In order to address the issue, the first step is to be aware of the importance of providing a safe, protected environment for students and staff in schools. Moving beyond awareness, schools still face the problem of *how* to provide effective initiatives that prevent violence and promote healthy relationships. Policies and interventions too often focus on controlling student behaviour through zero tolerance policies and harsh consequences for violations. As we have pointed out in our book, *Adolescent Risk Behaviour*[16], rules and enforcement are necessary and important, but they must be accompanied by developmentally relevant and proactive education to assist youth in healthy decision-making and harm avoidance.

For many students, schools are the first places where they spend time with people who are not friends or family. Students need an opportunity to learn about relationships and how to handle problems in relating with others in a non-violent manner. It is well-known that the early years of development are critically important for children to learn how to relate to others, but these important tasks continue to develop throughout childhood. Early adolescence also offers opportunities for growth and adjustment to new demands. For educators, it is important to understand that throughout all of the developmental stages, relationship patterns are adaptable and can be altered through appropriate educational strategies. Choosing the most

---

[16] Wolfe, D.A., Jaffe, P.G., & Crooks, C.V. (2006). *Adolescent risk behaviors*: *Why teens experiment and strategies to keep them safe.* New Haven, CT: Yale University Press.

appropriate prevention programs is critical for the development of students' ability to learn to prevent violence and develop healthy relationships.

WHAT ARE EDUCATORS LOOKING FOR IN VIOLENCE PREVENTION PROGRAMS?

Educators may wholeheartedly embrace the need for violence prevention in schools, but still feel overwhelmed by the number of available program options. Many questions emerge when considering programs and strategies to address violence prevention. How do you determine which option is most effective for your students, staff, and school community? Which programs are most effective in reaching students, staff, and parents? Who should be involved in developing your safe school plan? Are the policies, programs, and strategies in place at your school effective? How do you resolve competing interests and incorporate the ideas of multiple stakeholders and decision-makers?

Even within one school, different people will be focused on different aspects of a program. The school administrator may be looking at the big picture such as finding resources and investigating the research findings on various programs. In contrast, teachers may be more interested in details and pragmatics. Teachers want to know that a program addresses their students' needs first of all, and that the program produces the results it claims. Teachers also want to know how a new program or strategy will align with existing priorities.

A number of initiatives have documented the needs of school administrators in terms of implementing violence prevention programs. The two discussed in the following section are a survey of Ontario principals conducted by the Ontario Principal Council in conjunction with our research team, and a project conducted in Alberta by Leslie Tutty and her colleagues.

WHAT SUPPORT DO PRINCIPALS NEED?

OPC SURVEY OF PRINCIPALS

In the spring of 2005, our research team approached the Ontario Principal's Council (OPC) to conduct an online survey. The survey asked school administrators what support would assist them in implementing good, sustainable violence prevention programs in their school.

Over 300 principals and vice-principals, representing 31 school boards across the province, responded to the survey. Nearly three-quarters of the responses were from elementary school administrators.

The results of the online survey confirmed that determining the most effective and developmentally appropriate program, along with which programs meet their unique school needs, were challenges for school administrators. In fact, almost all of the school administrators who responded indicated that an inventory of available, effective violence prevention programs and assistance in identifying developmentally appropriate programs for each grade level would be valuable. Similarly, virtually all respondents agreed that identifying programs that match unique school needs would be helpful.

Over 95% of the school administrators who responded to the survey indicated that the following would be somewhat or very valuable:

Most administrators also indicated a desire for strategies to engage parents in violence prevention initiatives. Finally, nearly all of the administrators (87%) indicated that strategies to more actively engage students in violence prevention activities would be very valuable. Clearly the issue of engaging partners is paramount to administrators.

Research conducted by Leslie Tutty and Kendra Nixon of RESOLVE[17] Alberta indicates that it is a challenge to evaluate and select the most appropriate and effective violence prevention programs (Tutty & Nixon, 2000). The researchers surveyed school personnel to learn about prevention programs and what elements help them to decide which programs are appropriate for their school. The survey also asked which violence prevention programs were currently being used in the schools, and what they have used in the past. Over 600 surveys were returned and used in the data analysis. Tutty and Nixon reported that about one-third of the respondents found the information available on violence prevention programming confusing, both in terms of choosing appropriate programs and evaluating what constitutes an effective program. Many of the school personnel suggested that they do not have the background to assess program evaluation results. As a result, they don't know what to look for in a program that represents best practices.

The researchers also conducted in-depth telephone interviews with 17 members of the Children and Youth Subcommittee, a subcommittee of the Action Committee Against Violence. Beyond the issue of selecting an appropriate program, these interviews identified many systemic barriers faced in program implementation. The findings from these interviews indicate that some respondents were concerned about the ways in which programs are used to address the issue of violence prevention. Some felt that programs were being implemented inconsistently, while others were concerned that programs were not reaching all children and youth. In particular, respondents indicated that not all schools have access to these programs, and there are often long waiting lists for the better programs. The quality of programs was also questioned, since new programs are being introduced with little long-term planning and coordination. In particular, respondents were concerned that new programs are being developed without consultation with community agencies with expertise about the issue, or without identifying how the program will address the gaps in schools. Finally, lack of resources

---

[17] RESOLVE (Research and Education for Solutions to Violence and Abuse) is a research network located in Alberta, Manitoba, and Saskatchewan. It coordinates and supports research aimed at ending violence, particularly violence involving girls and women.

and lack of long-term funding of programs were identified as barriers to effective implementation.

WHAT DO EFFECTIVE PROGRAMS LOOK LIKE?

An important first step in identifying potential programs for your school is to understand the key characteristics of effective programs. Some prevention programs such as boot camps have gained considerable popularity because they sound good and promise a quick fix to youth violence. Unfortunately, the popularity of these approaches is not warranted by their evaluations, which indicate that they bring little or no benefit to youth. Characteristics of ineffective programs include insufficient duration, lack of developmentally appropriate focus, and mismatch with accepted theories of the development of violent behaviour. Furthermore, zero tolerance programs in isolation have not been found to be effective. Any programs that offer a quick fix should be viewed with skepticism. Violence is a complex phenomenon with many different contributors, and effective programs need to address these multiple factors.

In contrast, effective violence prevention programs are based on theoretically sound principles and research findings. Based on the Surgeon General's Report[18] and the Blueprints Violence Prevention Initiative,[19] successful programs:

- *Are comprehensive in nature:* Effective programs target multiple levels of influence, such as individuals, parents, school climate, and teacher training. They can also be comprehensive with respect to addressing overlapping risk behaviours (such as the *Life Skills Training* program which concurrently addresses substance use and violence). By definition a comprehensive approach suggests a reasonable duration, and cannot be achieved through single activities, such as a guest speaker or assembly alone;
- *Focus on skills:* Most typically communication and problem-solving skills are taught in effective programs. These programs use interactive, skill-based strategies (such as

---

[18] *Youth violence: A report to the surgeon general* (2000) is available at: http://www.surgeongeneral.gov/library/youthviolence/order.htm

[19] *Blueprints for violence prevention*, a project of the Center for the Study and Prevention of Violence at the University of Colorado, is an initiative to identify empirically validated violence prevention programs according to stringent criteria for what constitutes a "promising" or "best" practice. http://www.colorado.edu/cspv/blueprints/index.html

role play), and do not rely solely on information and didactic approaches to transfer skills;

- *Pick appropriate targets for change:* Effective programs target factors known to be related to the problem behaviour. Attitudes and skills, school connectedness, and coping skills are examples of appropriate prevention targets because they are all implicated in the development and use of violence. Bystander involvement is another excellent target because of the role played by bystanders in violence (particularly bullying);

- *Include peers in the delivery of the program:* Effective programs may include peer facilitators, a peer mentoring component or youth committee. The use of peers increases the salience of the material as youth identify more readily with these role models;

- *Include parents:* Although the extent and nature of appropriate parental involvement depends on the developmental stage of the youth, some parental involvement is regarded as a critical component for effective prevention programs. These components can range from parent sessions to information to parent-child components;

- *Attempt to change the larger environment:* Effective programs recognize the complex ecology of youths' lives and work to change these environments. For example, in school-based programming attempts to change the environment may include altering norms about help-seeking, and building the capacity of teachers and administrators to respond to violence.

- *Attend to implementation issues:* Effective programs understand that implementation issues are as critical as the program materials themselves. In the school setting, providing adequate resources for teacher training is essential. Furthermore, training needs to be ongoing rather than a one-time event to address teacher turnover and to prevent program drift.

Effective programs are a foundational piece of a comprehensive strategy to prevent violence in schools. However, good programs are not the only necessary component. Good policies and an attention to school climate are also key features of safe schools. Throughout this book we will address all of these components.

SUMMARY

In summary, the major challenge in choosing and implementing a safe schools initiative is not a lack of motivation. While administrators and staff may have different points of view, both are committed to ensuring that their students learn in a safe and secure learning environment. In this book, beginning with Chapter 4, we will outline a process for identifying specific safe school needs and planning to address those needs in a manner that involves administrators and teachers, as well as students, parents, and community members. Involving all partners in education is essential to the sustainability of safe schools and will assist in identifying strategies and programs that meet the needs of all partners at the table.

While choosing programs or strategies that meet the needs of all educational partners may seem a challenge, time spent working through the process outlined in the following chapters will put you on the road to future sustainability. You will find sample assessment tools and protocols, assistance with goal-setting strategies, sample policies, and information on effective, research-based programs that will allow you to develop and implement the most effective violence prevention strategies and programs for your school.

The challenge of choosing the most appropriate programs, reviewing and developing policies, and determining the next steps raises significant barriers to getting started on your safe schools plans. In fact, these challenges turn into an opportunity to carefully assess the school's safety needs, and to develop programming that responds to the identified needs. Through this process, many of the apparent challenges of choosing safe school programs and strategies may well be resolved. Through our research, we have found that there are barriers that commonly plague the implementation process, but knowing some challenges at the outset can help you begin to develop a plan. These challenges will be reviewed in the following chapter.

It is important to be aware of potential barriers to implementing and sustaining a violence prevention strategy. Recognizing that there are some universal challenges and not just a problem with *your* school, *your* students, or *your* community partners is a helpful starting place. It is sometimes difficult to anticipate challenges, but focusing on the positive opportunities may help you to overcome these unforeseen barriers that arise along the way. In this chapter, we will examine some of the typical barriers and challenges you may encounter. We will start by clarifying what we mean by *sustainable* change.

WHAT IS SUSTAINABLE CHANGE?

Sustainability means different things to different people. While many define sustainability simply as maintaining a program on an ongoing basis, it is much more than that.

> *Sustainability is the capacity of a system to engage in the complexities of continuous improvement consistent with deep values of human purpose.*[20]

Hargreaves and Fink put a similar emphasis on the capacity of a system to be self-sustaining and not preclude innovation.

> *Sustainability does not simply mean whether something will last. It also addresses how particular initiatives can be developed without compromising the development of others in the surrounding environment now and in the future.*[21]

For the purposes of this book, we see sustainability as embracing both concepts: the ongoing maintenance of a program, and the capacity to adapt to changing needs. Thus, sustainability is a commitment to an ongoing process rather than a specific outcome.

---

[20] Fullan, M. (2005). *Leadership and sustainability: System thinkers in action.* Thousand Oaks, CA: Corwin Press; Toronto: Ontario Principal's Council (p. ix).

[21] Hargreaves, A. & Fink D. (2000). The three dimensions of reform. *Educational Leadership*, April 2000, 30-34.

OUR PROJECT ON SUSTAINABLE STRATEGIES FOR SAFE SCHOOLS

Over a period of three years, we worked with 23 schools in four boards across Ontario as they navigated the implementation of strategies for violence prevention. During these three years we engaged in a consultation process with these schools. In the first year we visited schools to conduct an assessment and determine the unique needs of the school. We collected data in a variety of ways including brainstorming activities, surveys, and interviews. At a subsequent visit we summarized the assessment findings and engaged in a goal-setting process with administrators to identify goals congruent with the needs of their schools. These goals were established through our process of assessing the school's needs and applying a stage-based model of change, discussed in subsequent chapters. At following visits we assessed progress towards specific goals, as well as new challenges that had arisen. Thus, we were not only studying, but influencing the process of change undertaken by these schools.

Throughout the process we corresponded regularly to document and influence the changes taking place. We also interviewed principals or vice-principals on two occasions about what they felt facilitated sustainable change and what barriers and challenges they encountered. Emphasis was on their experience with sustainable change and, in particular, on their experience with using a process-oriented approach to assessing their school's needs. In an attempt to share the rich experiences of the administrators captured in this process, we quote them to illustrate key ideas throughout the remainder of our book.

WHAT ARE THE BARRIERS IN CREATING SUSTAINABLE CHANGE?

We have identified eight themes that consistently arose when talking to administrators about barriers and challenges to sustainability of safe schools programs.

BARRIER #1: POLICIES THAT CAN ACCOMMODATE DIVERSITY ACROSS COMMUNITIES

> *I looked at the challenges that they (Provincial of Education) would face, the breadth and scope of the problem. How do you collect data? How do you understand the problem? There is urban versus rural. How do you account for cultural diversity? So, if you are developing a program, it may work in the south, but not in the north. Who do you put in charge? Where do you start? (Principal)*
>
> *Balancing issues of equity...creating legislation that is flexible enough to be fair; firm enough to be effective. (Principal)*

Principals told us that Ontario's great diversity of people—urban and rural, aboriginal and immigrant—presented a unique challenge to the formulation of policies and legislation. It was a challenge to form policies that were workable in all situations in their vast province. Likewise, the amalgamated district school boards covered vast geographic areas with diverse populations. For school administrators, provincial policies may not reflect the situation at their local school and often did not provide them with the flexibility they needed to take action at the school level.

BARRIER #2: DIVERSE NEEDS AND EXPERIENCES OF FAMILIES AND COMMUNITIES

> *I think they [parents] would like to have more involvement with creating anti-violence programs, but they are constrained because they have to put food on the table for their kids. Many parents at our school don't have jobs, or have low paying jobs which limit their time and energy for involvement in school. (Principal)*
>
> *Back home you were allowed to hit. Back home a parent would go to the school, tell them the problem and the school would take care of it. Understanding the system here is huge for our parents. (A principal with a large population of new Canadians in her school)*

Principals indicated that the diverse needs of their communities and the differing understanding of the school's role create challenges to sustaining safe school programs. In some communities, parents almost expect the school to raise their child. In other communities where there are large immigrant populations, the principals find that there is a different understanding of the school's role and response to situations (e.g., physical punishment is acceptable to some).

Trying to change deeply-entrenched values is a complex problem. Principals' perceptions about the engagement of parents in the implementation and sustainability of safe schools reflect this complexity. Many parents are overwhelmed in our society. Many are raising their children single-handedly, many are in a cultural milieu that is new to them, and many struggle to put food on the table. While the importance of literacy and numeracy is obvious to them, it is easier to overlook the importance of safe schools issues that are by nature complex and whose influence on learning is less obvious.

BARRIER #3: CONFLICTING PRIORITIES FOR EDUCATORS

> *I think that the challenge is that they (school administrators) are forced into a reactive role most of the time, putting out fires. Once all the fires are put out, there isn't necessarily the time to do the proactive thing. (Principal)*
>
> *Time for staff and the myriad expectations that they are expected to carry out. I think there is a feeling of being overwhelmed. (Principal)*

Several principals noted that conflicting priorities and time are the most significant barriers to sustaining safe school initiatives. Principals spoke of the various initiatives that the Ministry of Education and their school boards were requiring of them. These initiatives are in many cases extremely important to improving the educational experience for children and youth. However, principals indicated that a safe school environment was one of the basic needs in the hierarchy of need for achievement; if schools are not safe and secure, learning will not take place. Nonetheless, with so many external factors pressing the principals for time, maintaining a focus on providing a safe school environment is a challenge. Forces conspire to keep principals in a reactive mode. Shifting from a reactive to a proactive mode requires huge effort and leadership skills.

BARRIER #4: TEACHERS' AND STUDENTS' PERCEPTIONS ABOUT RESPONSIBILITY FOR SAFE SCHOOLS

> *Some teachers feel a responsibility to this cause and others either don't or don't feel comfortable addressing the issue...Everyone agrees it is a problem but not everybody agrees that they have a role in fixing it or on what the right approach is to fix it. (Principal)*

Both teachers and students have slightly different but related issues with respect to understanding individual responsibility for safe schools. Principals indicated that they are not just implementing an academic program; they are also trying to change the school environment and change attitudes. In essence, they are tackling the difficult challenge of changing a culture. Some principals stated that this school culture is the most significant problem they encounter in trying to sustain violence prevention and safe schools programs.

The principals reported that the staff members feel the effects of the complexity of the issue of providing sustainable safe school environments. Most staff members are aware of the importance of safe schools. Events in recent years in Columbine, Taber, and Toronto have made everyone aware of the importance of maintaining a safe school environment and addressing violence prevention. However, confronted with the challenge of being the agents of change in the school, staff may fail to see that they have an integral role to play or be unsure about the nature of that role. Indeed, in many cases principals identified teacher attitudes in this respect as a barrier. According to principals, many teachers respond to safe school obligations by saying, "No, I am a teacher first." This issue is made even more complex by the demands of supervising students and the collective agreements to which teachers are bound. These safe school issues often become operationalized through the terms of employment emerging from labour negotiations.

The complexity of changing the culture of schools may be particularly challenging when it comes to engaging students in violence prevention programs. While many students acknowledge that there needs to be a change to a less violent culture, it becomes a challenge for them to assist and risk appearing "not cool" in front of their peers. When it comes to reporting incidents of bullying or aggressive behaviour on the part of their peers, it becomes a matter of their own personal safety in some instances, or at least not risking the disapproval of their peers. Principals confirmed that students struggle under the influence of society outside the school and the very different message they receive from school and their peers.

BARRIER #5: PERVASIVE SOCIETAL MESSAGES ABOUT THE ACCEPTABILITY OF VIOLENCE

Most of our students grow up in a cultural milieu of violence as seen on T.V., news, day to day life. There is a clash of values between what we promote as being good citizens vs. what students see out there and how problems are solved in the real world. (Principal)

Speaking of parents, I think one of the biggest challenges is their lack of understanding of why it is such an important issue for schools to address. The whole mentality of boys will be boys. (Principal)

Faced with the complexity of the issue, our principals pointed to society at large and the cultural milieu in which their students spend the bulk of their time. Principals referred to the fact that the students were only in school for a few hours a day. They reported feeling overwhelmed by what kids are exposed during the other 18 hours a day. When asked about the barriers that students face, or that they face when dealing with students, more than half of the principals reported that mixed messages from school as opposed to the home are a real challenge in implementing and sustaining safe schools programs.

The attribution of external forces as a challenge to implementing and sustaining safe schools programs is well documented in the literature on school change. Dufour and colleagues[22] used the term "external focus" which they identified as "looking at the conditions outside of the organization that impede its progress or success" as a barrier to an action. They agree that educators must continue to confront society with the sense of urgency they feel regarding the situations they face at school, but they must also accept and acknowledge that there are things that they can do within their school to influence and educate students. In fact, they state that educators can have a much more powerful influence than any external factors. We do not intend to minimize the very real challenges facing families, but despite these realities, educators need to be able to focus on making things better.

BARRIER #6: SHORTAGE OF RESOURCES

I think one of the biggest challenges to maintaining a safe school is that in our school with over 1000 students, we have only one vice principal in charge of discipline...It seems ironic: some schools have had reductions in vice principals at the same time as we are supposed to be working on safe schools. (Principal)

Support for guidance. I think the barrier for students is that they have no one to go to. Maybe with someone—instead of lashing out in class because he/she is angry, is if they had someone they could go to and speak with that would take the burden off his/her shoulders...If you carry it around all day, you just drop it at some point. (Principal)

The issue of having enough resources including funds, programs, and materials was repeatedly mentioned by all of the partners in the context of safe schools programming. Principals spoke of the limited resources available to them as the most significant barrier their

---

[22] Dufour R., Eaker, R., & Dufour, R. (2005). Closing the Knowing-Doing Gap. In R. Dufour, R. Eaker & R. Dufour (Eds.), *On Common Ground* (225-254) Bloomington, Indiana: National Educational Service.

community partners face in assisting schools to be safe. Principals receive strong support from the community, especially police services, but they acknowledged that these agencies are stretched thinly due to lack of financing and the resulting lack of personnel and resources. Principals spoke of long waiting lists and programs that are inaccessible due to distance or lack of resources. Some principals referred to the fact that there are fewer agencies in rural areas than in urban. However, principals in urban areas also felt that there were not enough agencies or resources in existing agencies to serve their students.

The Provincial Ministry of Education was seen as being the potential source of additional funds and materials to aid in maintaining strong violence prevention programs. Several principals mentioned that the ministry could be more effective not only in providing resources, but also in how resources are provided. Some principals spoke with frustration about getting "money bombs" – opportunities for significant funds that seem to appear out of nowhere and are tied to very specific mandates. With these money bombs, school boards are expected to complete applications for funding opportunities within very short timeframes. These funding opportunities frequently do not relate to the board's priorities and planning and, in fact, discourage good planning and integration by the school boards.

Concerns were also raised about the need for additional staff resources at the school level. Principals feel that an additional vice principal, a resource teacher, or a guidance teacher is needed to assist them to shift from a reactive position to a proactive position in terms of providing a safe school environment.

I have one hour a month to inform the staff of what is going on, including professional development and all that is going on, and anti-bullying...We need more time with our staff. That is way bigger than money. Way bigger...I don't struggle with money things. (Principal)

Training for staff. How can I ensure that my staff members are all delivering the same message using common language? (Principal)

At the heart of any learning community is the opportunity for development and renewal of staff and administration. Principals identified the need for resources and time for professional development as a major barrier to sustainability of safe schools programs. Without the resources to pay to train staff in safe schools initiatives and programs, it is difficult to sustain the programs that are in place, especially considering that staff will change year to year. Some principals pointed to the provincial framework negotiated between the Ontario government and the teachers' federations as a barrier to finding the time for professional development.

The school administrators who responded to the Ontario Principals' Council survey endorsed the importance of professional development in violence prevention. A total of 97% of respondents felt that professional development opportunities were somewhat valuable or very valuable to assist with implementing sustainable violence prevention programs. Equally important in the administrators' view is the opportunity for professional development for school administrators, with 98% responding that it is somewhat or very valuable.

> *I think one of the issues is administrative transfers. I am very interested in bullying, but I may get transferred this year. It is the continuity, starting programs and keeping them sustained. (Principal)*
>
> *Turnover in administration is an issue with a lot of these changes...All the studies; people like Fullan, all suggest it won't happen overnight. It takes about five years to get some of these changes embedded in the culture. Being able to maintain administrative complement is a help. (Principal)*

Administrative turnover is a reality for many schools. We witnessed the upheaval caused by turnover firsthand during this consultation process. Of the 23 schools participating in the project, six experienced a change in principal in the first year of the project. One school has had three principals in the past year. Even in schools where there has been some succession planning, it takes principals a few months to adjust fully to a new school and to turn their attention to ongoing projects. Every time there was a changeover, our project was delayed or slowed down. It is reasonable that this adjustment period affects all ongoing initiatives within a school and likely the school's overall effectiveness.

Turnover also affects staff members and, in some cases, the loss of a key staff member can provide a significant blow to a safe schools program. In one of our participating schools, the peer mediation program is on hold for a year until the teacher who had training in peer mediation returns from maternity leave. No other staff member was able to fill the gap for a year. Principals spoke of the need for succession planning to prepare for the loss of a significant staff leader.

SUMMARY

In this chapter we have identified numerous barriers that administrators face in developing, implementing, and sustaining safe schools. Labelling these barriers is an important step in the process. Anticipating these challenges helps prepare administrators to maintain their focus and the overall planning process. Understanding the reality of the landscape in which you are working is an important starting point. The reality is that many good teachers transfer to other schools, social programs are underfunded, and educators have a million competing priorities. That is the backdrop against which you are attempting to develop and implement a comprehensive safe schools plan. In the next chapter we introduce a framework for action in the context of understanding the change process.

While the barriers outlined in the previous chapter may appear daunting, they need not be impediments to the change process. Awareness of these potential pitfalls is useful in assessing your school's situation and identifying growth opportunities. In this and subsequent chapters, we will outline a process for developing a framework for action that will assist you in articulating your school's unique needs and choosing appropriate next steps. There is no one-size-fits-all solution to violence prevention. You need to take the time to work with your school community to assess your school's unique safe school needs and develop a plan tailored to respond to those identified needs. In this chapter we describe a *stages of change* model that depicts the process by which schools can integrate safe schools strategies in a sustainable manner. We illustrate three stages with school profiles that have been adapted from our partner schools to illustrate some of the successes and challenges typical at each stage of change. The actual names of the schools have been changed.

Change is not a one step process. It involves a series of transitions along the way from recognizing the presence of a problem to achieving sustainable change. One model that is well supported by empirical evidence is the Transtheoretical Model of Change (TTM) which was developed to provide a framework to understanding small but important changes that take place within an individual who makes a major change in health-related behaviours.[23]

THE TRANSTHEORETICAL MODEL OF CHANGE (TTM)

The TTM is based on the theory that individuals go through a series of stages when they embark on a change in behaviour, such as the cessation of smoking. Each stage in the process differs from the previous stage in terms of an individual's readiness to take action. Individuals, generally, do not move through these stages in a linear manner, but rather have some occasional slippage to the previous stage before moving forward again. Recognizing that this

---

[23] Prochaska, J.O.; DiClemente, C.C., (1982). Transtheoretical therapy: Toward a more integrative model of change. *Psychotherapy: Theory, research & practice, 19*, 276-288. For a more thorough description of the development and various applications of the Transtheoretical Model of Change see the Prochange website www.prochange.com

slippage is part of the change process helps individuals plan for such relapses, rather than allowing themselves to be derailed by these setbacks. Research supports that matching particular strategies to the individual's stage of change improves the success rates and decreases the chance of the individual dropping out across a wide range of targeted behaviours. For example, someone who is just beginning to think about whether he might want to stop smoking might be overwhelmed and easily discouraged by a complex behavioural program requiring tracking and homework. This individual might be better served by opportunities to discuss the pros and cons of quitting and to resolve his ambivalence. On the other hand, someone who has given the issue a lot of thought and is really committed to smoking cessation and has a start date in mind would likely benefit from a detailed program and find open-ended discussion about the pros and cons of quitting to be a waste of time.

In the TTM model, the first stage of change is a pre-contemplation stage, in which individuals are not thinking about changing their behaviour and may be in denial about the extent of the problem. In the contemplation stage, the individual is aware that they have a problem and they intend to make a change in the near future. It is when the person reaches the preparation stage that they make plans to take immediate action. By the action stage, an individual is making specific behavioural changes. Once the behavioural change is made and become integrated into everyday living, the person has reached the final stage – maintenance. As noted, this model does not conceptualize change as a linear process with an endpoint, and even individuals in the maintenance stage may need to do work in different stages if they experience some backsliding.

APPLYING THE TRANSTHEORETICAL MODEL

The Transtheoretical Model was applied originally as a model for describing change in health-related behaviour, but has subsequently been expanded to address change in social issues including violence perpetration. The model successfully explains change in a wide range of behaviours. In addition, the model has been applied to organizations. A new initiative's success may depend on whether the implementation was attempted with the organization's readiness to adopt the change being addressed.

Although the Transtheoretical Model of Change provides a useful framework for change, it requires some modification and adaptation to fit school-based prevention initiatives. Our adaptation is a three-stage change model to describe the progression of schools with relation to achieving integrated and sustainable safe schools initiatives.[24] We refer to this model as the Safe Schools Continuum and it includes stages called Developing Awareness; Planning and Responding; and, Educating and Leading. The model was revised throughout this project based on our work with 23 schools and other educational partners to ensure that it is a model that makes sense and confers benefit to administrators and their teams. Each stage has particular characteristics, attitudes and actions associated with it, which assist educators in locating their particular school along the Safe Schools Continuum (see Table 1).[25]

The utility of the Safe Schools Continuum is that awareness of your school's current place on the continuum helps you to identify concrete actions that are likely to be successful in moving your school to the next stage. Developing and implementing a safe school plan requires an investment of time and talent from a wide range of school partners. As a leader you can inadvertently set your school up for failure by attempting a complicated intervention without the necessary foundation or sufficient buy-in from partners. A school that is not yet ready to take on an extensive violence prevention program may be better served by developing smaller interventions and prevention initiatives that will assist the school to build the momentum needed to address the larger issues. Based on a school's readiness for change as described in the Safe Schools Continuum, different strategies and programs may be appropriate at your school.

You will want to better understand the Safe Schools Continuum before bringing your school partners together to determine how to proceed with your violence prevention initiatives. There are clear advantages to using the Safe Schools Continuum to conceptualize your school's needs. You will have the benefit of a model that informs your understanding of your school's readiness

---

[24] This work stems from earlier work by Sudermann, M., Jaffe, P.G. & Hastings, E. (1993). *ASAP: A school-based anti-violence program*. London Family Court Clinic. The authors also acknowledge the early work of administrator Deb Homuth in articulating the three stages and defining characteristics of each.

[25] Table 1 is a condensed version of the original stages of change model which outlines the characteristics and programs associated with each stage of change.

to change and provides guidelines based on empirically supported ideas about working with resistance to change. The use of this model along with the process outlined in later chapters to assess your school's needs will assist you in meeting your schools needs at your current place on the change continuum. By taking the time to identify your school's needs and your stage of change on the Safe Schools Continuum, there will be less likelihood of overwhelming your school partners, including staff, students and parents, and inadvertently fuelling their resistance to change.

The three stages are described in the following paragraphs. For each stage we provide a summary adapted from the schools in our study (although the school names have been changed). These summaries were generated after our first consultation visit and illustrate the characteristics representative of each stage, as well as some preliminary planning that was undertaken to identify suitable next steps. This assessment and planning process will be detailed in subsequent chapters, but these summaries provide an initial overview.

In the Stages of Change model there are three stages with transitions between each stage. Below is a description of each stage and its salient characteristics.

Stage One: *Developing Awareness*
- Characteristics of this stage include the following:
  - *Small number involved*
  - *Many still wanting to bury the crisis*
  - *Low profile in the school*
  - *Resources not identified*
- The following actions & attitudes characterize this stage:
  - *Naming the problem, measuring, assessing, auditing, examining, surveying, reading, investigating.*
- Programs associated with this stage: *Videos, assemblies, motivational speakers, one time events*

Moving to Stage Two: *Transition stage* - While some of the characteristics of stage one are still present, there is some movement toward stage two.

Stage Two: *Planning & Responding*
- Characteristics of this stage include the following:
  - ***More educational partners involved,*** *higher profile for violence prevention activities, more people are understanding, still depends on outside resources*
- The following actions and attitudes characterize this stage:
  - *Engaging, developing, implementing, meeting, reinforcing, creating, modifying, training staff, planning, understanding the problem & making the links to gender, race or vulnerabilities, developing action plans, wanting to involve all stakeholders, hopeful about potential for change, accepting challenges*
  - *Programs associated with this stage: Kelso's Choices, Character Education, partial implementation of some more comprehensive programs, programs are additional to the curriculum.*

Moving to Stage Three: *Transition stage* - While some of the characteristics of stage two are still present, there is some movement towards stage three.

Stage Three: *Educating and Leading*
- Characteristics of this stage include the following:
  - ***The majority of educational partners are involved.*** *The school community is strongly supportive. Violence prevention is high profile in the school and well recognized, the school is generating resources to be shared.*
- The following actions and attitudes characterize this stage:
  - *Consolidating, leading, enhancing, staff to staff mentoring, student to student mentoring, sharing, evaluating, reviewing, celebrating, recognizing, rewarding, sustaining, taking responsibility for the problem, comfortable with all stakeholders at the table, no need to cover-up problem areas, willing to share expertise, believing in capacity to respond, dynamic, open to change.*
  - *Programs associated with this stage: Fourth R, programs embedded in the curriculum*

STAGE 1: DEVELOPING AWARENESS

Schools in the Developing Awareness stage recognize that bullying and violence in the school are issues that need to be addressed by all stakeholders. School administration and staff understand that students need a safe environment before they can begin to learn. There is recognition that much work needs to be done to address issues of violence in the school community. These schools realize that they are not where they want to be with respect to safe schools, but may be unclear about next steps. Also, they may face significant barriers that seem insurmountable, such as staff resistance about prioritizing safe schools, and external community factors. The focus for Stage 1 schools is on building a foundation and increasing motivation across all stakeholders to prepare for making and implementing an action plan.

In this stage, the administration and staff will begin to review and assess school policies and procedures to further understand what has already been written and done to improve school safety. Surveys may be completed with students, staff and parents to measure understanding of bullying and violence in the school community. In this stage, there is much reading, auditing, inquiring, and discussing about the nature of violence in the school and how to improve the school environment. After a thorough investigation of the current situation, questions are raised and an examination into possible next steps is initiated.

Stage 1 schools may have some safe schools initiatives underway (indeed in the current climate it would be unusual to find a school doing nothing!) but their initiatives tend to be isolated and not integrated into a larger plan. Furthermore, there may be relatively few students or staff involved and a general lack of support for these initiatives. In some cases Stage 1 schools may look busy, but they are not really moving forward.

Northwest Secondary School is located just outside a major urban centre. The school serves about 1000 students from the surrounding area, a population that is larger than that of the local village. Almost all students are transported by bus.

During our initial consultation visit we discovered that there were some successful initiatives for students in terms of leadership activities but these involved only a few students and there were still some pockets of resistance to safe school changes on the part of both the students and staff. During our visit to the school we observed a student sporting a t-shirt that read, "If you can read this, the chick on the back fell off." A vice-principal was heard to announce on the PA, "Get your ass in gear and get on the bus." Clearly, there was a lack of awareness of the nature of the messages being sent. Prior to our visit there had been some incidents such as setting fires in the hall or setting cars on fire in the parking lot and some isolated incidents of violent behaviour. While staff seemed to acknowledge the importance of having a safe school, they did not necessarily see that they have a role to play in making the school a safer place.

Northwest Secondary School had a vice-principal who was very aware of the need for a safe and secure school environment and was beginning to do some significant work to move the school forward. A Respect Club was a relatively recent addition to the school and the student members had implemented some awareness activities, such as hosting assemblies on safe schools issues and sponsoring student posters on bullying. A short survey of 35 students had been conducted at a leadership camp. The results of this survey identified verbal bullying as a prevalent problem at the school and an appropriate target for improving school climate. Some further surveys were being considered to assess student attitudes to safety and security at the school and identify areas where the students did not feel safe. Clearly, this vice-principal was moving in the right direction but could use some assistance to ensure that the school's needs were assessed and identified before selecting the appropriate strategies and programs to address those needs.

As part of our consultation process we conducted a focus group with students and another with staff, administration, parents and one community member. The focus groups were walked through a "fishbone" brainstorming process (detailed in the next chapter). The results of this exercise confirmed that the school needed to continue to work to develop awareness amongst all educational partners, including staff, students, parents and the community and goals were set that were appropriate for a school in Stage 1 (Developing Awareness). The following goals were developed:

- Focus on increasing awareness of staff, students and parents about bullying behaviour and other safe school-related issues, through assemblies for students that included follow-up activities in the classroom
- Provide staff training in identifying and responding to bullying behaviour
- Publish articles on safe schools in the school newsletter
- Provide parent evenings on safe school issues such as media violence, cyber-bullying and violence prevention
- Survey students in one class at each grade level and conduct focus groups to further assess the school's needs before developing a safe schools plan

The school was strongly encouraged to work towards forming a Safe Schools Team composed of staff, students, parents and community members, as soon as possible. They were reminded that the work of developing awareness and increasing the numbers of education partners who understood and supported the need for change had to come first before specific action plans could be developed and implemented.

STAGE 2: PLANNING AND RESPONDING

A school in the Planning and Responding stage has a better understanding of it needs and is in a position to use that information to plan and implement specific strategies. In Stage 2, a school is using information from the audits or surveys conducted and review of other schools' initiatives to develop appropriate violence prevention protocols and plans. The school is beginning to acquire resources, develop new strategies and implement programs to address the issue of bullying and other forms of violence.

A Stage 2 school is actively working to engage representatives from all stakeholder groups (staff, students, parents and community agencies), although the success of these engagement attempts may be varied. Indeed, parent engagement was identified throughout our study as an ongoing challenge facing most schools, (even those who were clearly Stage 3 schools in all other respects). In Stage 2, committees are formed to establish goals and to assist in the creation of an overall plan for making the school environment safe for all students. Moreover, these committees meet on a regular and predetermined basis, rather than on an as-needed basis or solely in response to critical incidents. Decisions are made to reinforce or modify current protocols and processes and training is put in place to support the plan and encourage the implementation of specific initiatives. There is consensus among partners with respect to the action plan. Results of the various initiatives are measured and modifications made if required. In this stage, one senses a great deal of hope and energy on the road to the development of sustainable programs.

Riverside Elementary School is a large K-8 school in an urban area offering both English and French immersion programs. Students from the Junior and Intermediate Behaviour classes are integrated into a number of regular programs. About 25% of the students come from homes where English is spoken as a second language.

In its ongoing effort to develop awareness of school safety, Riverside had a number of initiatives underway targeting policies and programs. The students had recently completed a comprehensive school survey that included eleven questions on school climate. As well, regular safe school assemblies were embedded into the school calendar. A parent section on the school web site links to a variety of resources on topics which include internet safety and parenting skills. Staff was aware that there may be additional resources available through the school board, although they were not aware of what is available.

At the time of our first consultation visit, Riverside had a number of structures, policies, and activities in place that defined it as a predominantly Stage 2 school. Some of these initiatives were working well, while others had some room for further improvement. A committee of staff and administrators was meeting on safe school issues (albeit on an as needed basis). The group had specific actions outlined, and was preparing a safety binder for staff use. Stakeholders agreed that teachers generally maintained and enforced safe schools policies. When students were referred to the office, an office referral form was completed. Behaviour codes and dress codes were implemented and considered to be working well. There was a system in place to recognize and reward positive student behaviour, but there was a need to enhance and raise the profile of this award program. A bullying prevention program was in place, although the staff felt that improvement was needed in this program. At the time of our first visit the program included classroom lessons and assemblies. The class work emphasized a common vocabulary that included the following core values: communication, cooperation, courtesy, respect, responsibility, resolution. Senior students were assisting on the school yard as patrollers and there was a reading buddies program in place that enabled senior students to assist younger students. A local community agency offered a breakfast program to Riverside students. Roots of Empathy was implemented in the school.

In working with the Riverside administrator to identify steps that would help move the school to the Educating and Leading Stage in the safe school continuum, the following goals were established:

- Enhance the current award system to recognize positive student contributions to creating a safe school environment and give it a high profile within the school and community

- Enhance the bullying prevention program and make it more integrated into school activities in and out of the classroom

- Expand the staff and administrative safe schools committee to include representatives from all support staff groups, parents, senior students and community members

- Hold regular meetings of the safe schools committee (three times a year) to review and evaluate all aspects of school safety and to ensure sustainability of all safe school programs

STAGE 3: EDUCATING AND LEADING

A school at the Educating and Leading stage of the continuum has consolidated its safe schools efforts. The focus is on further integrating initiatives and maintaining a sense of renewal with them. New initiatives tend to be enhancements of existing programs and not stand alone programs. There is a diversification of effort in that no strategy undertaken as part of the safe school program is dependent on any single individual or small group of staff, but rather is embedded in the school curriculum and climate.

Staff, students, parents, and community partners readily take responsibility for the existence and implementation of a safe school environment. There is recognition that the maintenance of a safe and welcoming environment requires an active, ongoing commitment to review, evaluate, and respond to what is happening in the school and to share expertise with others beyond the school. Violence prevention and safe school initiatives are well integrated into all aspects of school life. The school has the capacity to respond effectively to any new issues which arise. Successes are celebrated and new staff, students, and parents are mentored as future leaders. At this stage the school is a role model of a dynamic safe school and is willing to share its experiences and expertise.

Despite their leadership and commitment to safe schools initiatives, Stage 3 schools are not without critical incidents or violence. What demarcates a Stage 3 school is the *response* to these incidents rather than a lack of them. Responses to violence are consistent and coordinated, and each of the stakeholders knows their role in these situations.

Lakeview Elementary School has an enrolment of just under 400 students. The school serves a small village and a rural community which includes three First Nations Communities.

All stakeholders at this school were aware of the need to address violence prevention and showed a commitment towards ongoing changes and enhancements to make their school safe and secure. This commitment is an ongoing one that includes a succession planning component directed towards ensuring that new staff members, students, parents and community members are made aware of the need for violence prevention and safe school programs.

In addition to meeting all of the requirements of a Stage 2 school, Lakeview could be characterized as a Stage 3 school because it had moved beyond the Planning and Responding phase in many regards. For example, the components listed as Stage 2 initiatives (above) were highly integrated into the school program and there was a process of ongoing renewal. The school was engaged in many strategies and programs that indicate that it was a Stage 3 school—Educating and Leading:

- Staff integrated different approaches to dealing with violence into the school program.

- Staff acted as a positive influence for students and was sensitive to different cultures.

- The school had a sophisticated student recognition system that celebrates positive behaviours and student participation in preventing violence

- Suspensions were used as a teaching opportunity. The administration attempted to provide natural consequences for children that reflected their misdemeanour.

- Students were actively involved in the Community Builders program and were beginning to do workshops in other schools.

- There was a high level of parent involvement at the school. Parents assisted as artists in the classrooms, snack volunteers, head lice checkers, field trip excursion volunteers, Home and School, and School Council.

While Lakeview had addressed many of the features of Stage 3, the school needed to continue to review and evaluate its safe schools practices. Through the initial consultation process, the following goals were identified:

- Develop a higher profile for positive student leadership in the school

- Continue to encourage parents and community representatives to have more input into violence prevention policy and leadership groups

- Promote and share programs and strategies with the local community and with other schools in the District School Board

The preceding profiles describe three very different schools. They have different demographics, different local assets, and challenges, and different priorities identified by their administrators. Clearly the violence prevention strategies working at one school might not work at the others. In addition, each of these three schools is currently in a different stage of change. Understanding the current stage and identifying realistic goals to move the school forward are more likely to be successful than overwhelming partners by scrambling to institute any and all initiatives.

It should be reiterated that change does not always move forward in a straight line from developing awareness to the third stage of educating and leading. Schools will experience setbacks – loss of key staff, critical incidents, funding cutbacks – before they are able to move forward again. Much like the game of Snakes and Ladders, where occasionally the player slides back down before being able to move forward again, so schools may experience back-sliding and must be constantly reviewing, evaluating and making adjustments to their safe schools strategies and programs to keep moving forward in a sustainable, integrated manner.

As an administrator, it is important to remember that not all of your partners will necessarily be at the same stage as another partner. You may find that students are already very aware of the need for violence prevention and are quite ready to move towards planning and responding, while your staff may, in fact, still need more information and education to get on board. You may want to address the staff needs through professional development and awareness activities. In any case, it is important to involve all of your educational partners in developing your violence prevention strategies and to recognize the needs of each group as they move along the safe schools continuum. The challenge is to maximize the strengths of a stakeholder group without abandoning another stakeholder that is further behind. Ultimately, the best sustainability is achieved only when all stakeholders are maximally engaged.

SUMMARY

In this chapter we have outlined our stages of change model as a way to help you conceptualize where your school may be on the *Safe Schools Continuum.* We provided examples of three schools with very different characteristics and needs, each of which would benefit from different types of strategies. In the next chapters, we will outline a model that will assist you to assess your school's needs through audits, surveys and focus groups, to develop a plan to address those needs, to implement those changes and then to consolidate or maintain them. By approaching your safe schools needs through a process-based approach, you will ensure that you have laid the groundwork that will enable you to select the right strategies and programs to move your school forward towards sustainable and integrated safe school strategies and programs.

> *The integrity of the implementation process affects sustainability: Shortcuts up front invariably lead to threats to sustainability. Example: Schools that go straight to program selection without developing a shared understanding of student needs, or that fail to involve teachers in program selection, can find half-hearted support and a short life for the intervention.*[26]

In the previous chapter we provided an overview of the change process as it relates to undertaking safe school initiatives. In this chapter we examine the starting point in this process, which involves an effective assessment of your school and the unique challenges that may be present. To a large extent, sustainability of your safe school initiatives depends on your approach to assessing your schools needs. This assessment provides the foundation for everything that follows. The assessment process you use should involve an assessment of your school's needs and strengths through multiple methods such as surveys, focus groups, and checklists. The development and implementation of safe schools' goals is based on the outcome of this assessment. In this chapter we describe the School Assessment Checklist, which is an assessment tool that will give you a profile of your strengths and weaknesses in the different domains of safe school planning (i.e., policies and procedures, interventions, preventions, and school climate). We describe a number of ways in which this checklist can be used. However, the completion of one checklist or survey will not achieve the comprehensive results you need as a foundation for your safe school plan. In the next chapter we describe a range of assessment methods through which your initial School Assessment Checklist results can be augmented.

There are many approaches to assessing your school's needs. As a starting point, you may consider completing the School Assessment Checklist found in Table 2 on the following

---

[26] O'Brien, M.U. (2006). *Implementing school-wide social and emotional learning (SEL) for student success.* Workshop presentation at the Safe Schools and Healthy Learnings Conference. St. Cloud, MN. Nov. 8, 2006. Available on-line at www.casel.org

pages. The checklist was designed in collaboration with principals across Ontario to assist in the assessment of a school's violence prevention programs, interventions, school climate and safe school policies and procedures. It can be completed by one individual or by more than one as described below. It can be done in your first meeting with your school safety committee or can be used later in the process. Several methods of using and scoring the template are described here so that you may consider how it will fit best into your process.

THE SCHOOL ASSESSMENT CHECKLIST

The School Assessment Checklist contains 41 items addressing four components of safe schools policies and procedures, interventions, prevention programs and school climate. The five-point scale corresponds to the three stages of change and two transition stages between them. The checklist will assist you to identify your school's needs in each area and through the use of the scoring guide will assist you to identify which stage of change best describes your school's progress in these four key areas. The profile of your school developed through scoring the School Assessment Checklist should assist you to identify areas where you need to focus your attention, as well as areas that you need to take time to enhance and celebrate.

INTRODUCTION TO THE SCHOOL ASSESSMENT CHECKLIST

Purpose of the Checklist

The checklist is a tool to gather information about your school across a variety of safe school areas such as the presence of safe school intervention strategies and the knowledge of safe school policies by staff and students. It has been designed to guide discussion and thinking at your school about the quality and nature of the strategies in place that contribute to a safe school. The checklist contains 41 items that show the many components that contribute to a safe and well-functioning school. Using it will enable school staff, students, parents and others to assess school needs, identify the stage that characterizes the school, and also identify next steps.

Completing the Checklist

Each school should decide the best way to complete the School Assessment Checklist. How you approach this important activity at your school depends on a number of factors including:

- What you hope to accomplish with the exercise
- The level of expertise and interest at the school
- Current level of staff, student, and community involvement
- The time available, and
- How urgent the problems are.

The research project identified two common approaches:

1. Based on extensive knowledge of the school and several years' experience there, some principals chose to complete the checklist on their own as the starting point for discussion at the school.
2. Other schools chose to provide a copy of the checklist to all members of the school team. Team members assessed each item either individually or as part of a group. The results were analyzed to come up with an overall assessment.

No matter how you complete the checklist, it will provide important information and direction as school staff, safe school committees, and partners work towards identifying needs sustaining improvement.

In the Stages of Change model, there are three stages with transitions between each stage. Below is a description of each stage and its key characteristics. Please read this section carefully before completing the questionnaire.

Stage	Name	Description
Stage One	*Developing Awareness*	**CHARACTERISTICS OF THIS STAGE INCLUDE THE FOLLOWING:** Small number of people involved; the school responds to crisis; violence prevention is generally low profile; resources are not identified. **THE FOLLOWING ACTIONS AND ATTITUDES CHARACTERIZE THIS STAGE:** Naming the problem, measuring, assessing, auditing, examining, surveying, reading, investigating. **PROGRAMS ASSOCIATED WITH THIS STAGE:** Videos, assemblies, motivational speakers, one-time events.
Moving to Stage Two	*Transition stage*	While some of the characteristics of stage one are still present, there is some movement toward stage two.
Stage Two	*Planning and Responding*	**CHARACTERISTICS OF THIS STAGE INCLUDE THE FOLLOWING:** More educational partners involved; higher profile for violence prevention activities; more people understand the issues; efforts still depend on outside resources. **THE FOLLOWING ACTIONS AND ATTITUDES CHARACTERIZE THIS STAGE:** Engaging; developing; implementing; meeting; reinforcing; creating; modifying; training staff; planning; understanding the problem and making the links to gender, race or vulnerabilities; developing action plans; wanting to involve all stakeholders; being hopeful about potential for change; accepting challenges. **PROGRAMS ASSOCIATED WITH THIS STAGE:** Kelso's Choices, Character Education, partial implementation of other comprehensive programs. Programs are additional to the curriculum.
Moving to Stage Three	*Transition stage*	While some of the characteristics of stage two are still present, there is some movement towards stage three.
Stage Three	*Educating and Leading*	**CHARACTERISTICS OF THIS STAGE INCLUDE THE FOLLOWING:** The majority of education partners are involved. The school community is strongly supportive. Violence prevention is high profile in the school and well recognized. The school is generating resources to be shared. **THE FOLLOWING ACTIONS AND ATTITUDES CHARACTERIZE THIS STAGE:** Consolidating; leading; enhancing; staff-to-staff mentoring; student-to-student mentoring; sharing; evaluating; reviewing; celebrating; recognizing; rewarding; sustaining; taking responsibility for the problem; being comfortable with all stakeholders at the table; not needing to cover-up problem areas; willing to share expertise **PROGRAMS ASSOCIATED WITH THIS STAGE:** Fourth R and other programs are embedded in the curriculum.

TABLE 2: STEP 2 – SCHOOL ASSESSMENT CHECKLIST

Please identify the Stage of Change that characterizes your school for each item. Place a ✓ under the Stage that corresponds to each item. In order to identify safe school strategies that address your school's unique needs, it is important to answer the questions accurately and honestly. The completion of this Checklist by different stakeholders may be useful in gathering information about your school. Please note that the words in the items such as "know" and "recognize" have been carefully thought out to reflect the stages of change model. Staff refers to all adults in the school.

	Stage 1	Transition to Stage 2	Stage 2	Transition to Stage 3	Stage 3
1. Students know the expectations of a safe school environment.					
2. Staff maintains a high level of visibility in the halls and school yard.					
3. Staff recognize that harassment and bullying are important issues for schools to address.					
4. Parents recognize that harassment and bullying are important issues for schools to address.					
5. Students recognize that harassment and bullying are wrong.					
6. Violence prevention issues are addressed in school newsletters and web sites.					
7. The school has a collection of violence prevention resources that are used regularly by staff.					
8. The school provides healthy sexuality, alcohol, and drug prevention programs.					
9. New staff, students, and parents are mentored as future leaders.					
10. Students are aware of the importance of school-based violence prevention initiatives.					
11. Students have an opportunity to participate in violence prevention initiatives.					
12. Violence prevention and safe school initiatives are well integrated into all aspects of school life.					
13. Violence prevention initiatives are integrated into the curriculum.					
14. Staff participate/have participated in violence prevention training.					
15. Students, staff, and parents meet regularly to keep issues of violence prevention moving forward.					
16. Staff are committed to implementing all recent board and Ministry of Education safe school policies.					
17. There is a protocol in place to allow students and parents to report incidents of bullying/harassment without fear of retaliation.					
18. The school makes efforts to share its violence prevention protocols with parents and other schools.					
19. Parents understand safe school policies and procedures.					
20. The Code of Conduct is well known by staff, students and parents.					
21. Staff consistently enforce the existing Code of Conduct.					

	Stage 1	Transition to Stage 2	Stage 2	Transition to Stage 3	Stage 3
Please identify the Stage of Change that characterizes your school for each item. Place a ✓ under the Stage that corresponds to each item. In order to identify safe school strategies that address your school's unique needs, it is important to answer the questions accurately and honestly. The completion of this Checklist by different stakeholders may be useful in gathering information about your school. Please note that the words in the items such as "know" and "recognize" have been carefully thought out to reflect the stages of change model. Staff refers to all adults in the school.					
22. The Code of Conduct meets the needs of the diverse student population.					
23. Staff members are confident and comfortable intervening in harassment and bullying incidents.					
24. When harassment and bullying reports are received, follow-up addresses the needs of both victims and perpetrators.					
25. A suspension re-entry program is established protocol for students suspended for violence.					
26. Students are trained and have an opportunity to use their non-violent conflict resolution skills.					
27. Information is readily available on how and where students can get help (e.g., in posters and planners).					
28. Both parents and students feel confident that reported incidents of violence will be addressed consistently by staff.					
29. Staff regularly describe, model, and reward respectful behaviour.					
30. Equity, social justice and other student clubs that support a safe school and promote respect and tolerance are well received by the school community.					
31. The physical plant is clean and well-cared for (e.g., graffiti are removed from the walls immediately).					
32. Staff recognize the underlying social factors associated with violence at school.					
33. Staff, students, and parents are actively involved on the safe schools committee (recommended in *Shaping Safer Schools, 2005*).					
34. The school is actively engaged in activities that encourage a sense of belonging and build school pride.					
35. Parents support violence prevention initiatives.					
36. The School Council see themselves as having an important role in violence prevention.					
37. Representatives of community agencies regularly make presentations on violence prevention issues in the school.					
38. Representatives of community agencies regularly attend and contribute to the safe schools committee.					
39. The Student Council supports violence prevention initiatives in the school.					
40. Students take initiative to access information and resources and actively participate in safe schools programs.					
41. The school recognizes and/or celebrates positive contributions to violence prevention efforts.					

There are several ways to complete the School Assessment Checklist. Your choice of method will depend on many factors including expertise, interest, student and community involvement, time commitments, previous experience with completion of checklists, and urgency of need. Regardless of how the checklist is completed it will provide important information and direction as school staff, safe school committees, and partners work towards identifying needs and sustaining improvement. In using the checklist it should be noted that while there are three stages in our model, it is possible to be in transition between the phases on a particular item, resulting in a checklist with five possible response choices for each checklist item.

There are different methods for completing the checklist. One person can complete the checklist. The principal (or another lead educator) with extensive knowledge of the school, may wish to complete the checklist on his/her own as a beginning point for discussion at the school. The benefit of this approach is efficiency. This approach has its limitations in that support for change will be greater if all interested parties contribute to the discussion and identification of the next steps.

An alternative method is to have multiple people complete the checklist and build consensus on the results. For example, the school team could be convened and each team member provided with a copy of the checklist. Then in a consensus building exercise team members arrive at an agreed upon response to each of the checklist items. One summary checklist is then generated based on this consensus. This process will lead to a higher level of awareness among informants as individuals explain their points of view. Although it takes more time than completion by a single informant, it will help build momentum and commitment through the engagement process.

A third approach that you may use with a group is to have each member complete the checklist and then compile the results to get an average for each response. This method provides more representative data than can be generated by one informant, but does not confer the same motivational benefit as the consensus-building approach. In addition, this approach provides a range and variability of views. Of particular interest with this method is the identification of areas where there is the most variability as there will need to be some reconciliation of views before action planning can ensue.

SCORING THE SCHOOL ASSESSMENT CHECKLIST

Whether the checklist is completed by an individual or several individuals, it can be scored to generate a profile that will help you identify what stage of change your school is at in each of the four areas: Policies and Procedures; Intervention; Prevention; and School Climate. Using the information generated by completing and scoring the checklist, you can identify the stage of change that best describes your school's progress in each of the areas. Once you have identified the areas that may need some attention, you will be able to generate a more tailored action plan, as described in Chapter 6. It is critical to the sustainability of your safe school initiatives that the choice of strategy or program reflects your school's stage of change and demonstrated safe school needs.

SUMMARY

The School Assessment Checklist provides a good overview of your relative strengths and weaknesses in different areas. Depending on how you utilize the assessment, it might also identify areas where individuals' perspectives on strengths and weaknesses diverge. Used annually, it can assist with tracking progress and identifying areas that continue to be troublesome over time and these results can be integrated into your overall school improvement plan.

Your completed Checklist describes your school's stage of change for each of the four areas – Prevention, Policy and Procedures, Intervention, and School Climate. In order to get a more complete picture and to identify the next steps for your school, you need to complete the scoring exercise shown below.

- For each of the four areas count the number of check marks in each column.
- Multiply the total for each column by 1, 2, 3, 4 or 5 as shown below.
- Add the 5 scores to get a total score for each area.
- Transfer the total score for each area to the Stage of Change Profile on the next page using the directions provided on the template.

Prevention (checklist items 1 to 15).   <u>Score</u>

Number of checks in column 1 (Stage 1) = ___ times 1 = ____
Number of checks in column 2 (Trs to 2) = ___ times 2 = ____
Number of checks in column 3 (Stage 2) = ___ times 3 = ____
Number of checks in column 4 (Trs to 3) = ___ times 4 = ____
Number of checks in column 5 (Stage 3) = ___ times 5 = ____

TOTAL SCORE for Prevention   ____

Policy and Procedures (checklist items 16 to 22).   <u>Score</u>

Number of checks in column 1 (Stage 1) = ___ times 1 = ____
Number of checks in column 2 (Trs to 2) = ___ times 2 = ____
Number of checks in column 3 (Stage 2) = ___ times 3 = ____
Number of checks in column 4 (Trs to 3) = ___ times 4 = ____
Number of checks in column 5 (Stage 3) = ___ times 5 = ____

TOTAL SCORE for Policy and Procedures   ____

Intervention (checklist items 23 to 28).   <u>Score</u>

Number of checks in column 1 (Stage 1) = ___ times 1 = ____
Number of checks in column 2 (Trs to 2) = ___ times 2 = ____
Number of checks in column 3 (Stage 2) = ___ times 3 = ____
Number of checks in column 4 (Trs to 3) = ___ times 4 = ____
Number of checks in column 5 (Stage 3) = ___ times 5 = ____

TOTAL SCORE for Intervention   ____

School Climate (checklist items 29 to 41).   <u>Score</u>

Number of checks in column 1 (Stage 1) = ___ times 1 = ____
Number of checks in column 2 (Trs to 2) = ___ times 2 = ____
Number of checks in column 3 (Stage 2) = ___ times 3 = ____
Number of checks in column 4 (Trs to 3) = ___ times 4 = ____
Number of checks in column 5 (Stage 3) = ___ times 5 = ____

TOTAL SCORE for School Climate   ____

Identify Your School's Stage Of Change Profile

Use this template to summarize your school's stage of change for each area and determine appropriate next steps.

Use a vertical line "|" to mark the total score from each of the 4 areas, place 4 vertical lines on the scales below. Note that the line may be between two numbers – that's okay. You are trying to get an overall picture of the stage of change currently identified at your school.
For example, if the total score for Prevention was 42, the line would be in the Prevention Stage 2 box (yellow).

	Stage 1	Stage 2	Stage 3
Prevention	15 23 30	38 45 53	60 68 75
Policy and Procedures	7 11 14	18 21 25	28 32 35
Intervention	6 9 12	15 18 21	24 27 30
School Climate	13 20 26	33 39 46	52 59 65

Once you have completed this profile, go to the next section to find activities and programs for each area that are associated with the stage you have identified for your school.

In the last chapter you were introduced to the School Assessment Checklist, which can be used to provide a good overview of your school's strengths and weaknesses. The checklist on its own does not provide the depth of information for a strong and detailed school safety plan. In this chapter, we discuss a number of other data collection strategies that can be used to augment the information you have already collected. A comprehensive assessment plan also includes many partners. By being inclusive in this process you will make your educational partners aware of the need for the implementation of safe school strategies and programs and engage them in the process of change. The assessment process itself becomes a motivational force that will have a positive effect on the sustainability of your safe school plans. We begin by discussing the need for a Safe School Committee. This Committee plays a critical role in assessment, planning, implementation and sustainability of safe schools initiatives.

SAFE SCHOOL COMMITTEE

Once you, as principal, have made the commitment to review your school's safety, you will want to recruit some support from your school partners, including staff, students, parents, and community members. You will need to share information about your vision of a safe and secure school environment with your partners in education. Your enthusiasm and passion at this point is critical because you will need to inspire others to want to be involved in this initiative and to join a safe schools team to share leadership of this initiative with you.

You will need to identify the educational partners who you know will share your enthusiasm for making your school safer. You may have an existing staff and administrative committee that could be expanded into a full-fledged safe school committee with the addition of parent, student and community representatives. It is essential to include your non-teaching staff. For example, the custodial staff plays a significant role in keeping your school safe. We have found that principals who have a functioning safe school committee with all partners at the table are very pleased with the assistance they receive in goal setting, planning, and implementing safe school initiatives from their committee. Another important group to consider including on your committee is bus drivers. By engaging individuals to assist on the safe school committee, you are going a long way to ensuring that your safe school initiatives will be sustainable. One of the hallmarks of sustainability is that many people are involved and committed. In many jurisdictions, having a safe school committee is required by government policy. For example in Ontario, provincial policy as outlined in Ontario Public Policy Memorandum 144 (October, 2007) requires that you have "a safe schools team responsible for school safety that is composed of at least one student (where appropriate), one parent, one teacher, one support staff member, one community partner, and the principal." Many District School Boards across the country require that each school have a school safety committee. Even if such a committee is not currently legislated, it constitutes best practice. Depending on the make-up of your school community, you may need to employ specific strategies to engage parents, such as through the provision of childcare during meetings, or scheduling meetings for certain times.

MAKING YOUR COMMITTEE WORK

Although a safe schools committee is important and possibly mandated, involving parents remains a challenge for many educators. Some committees exist in name only which is a lost opportunity for genuine collaboration. One of the principals involved in our project articulated a formula for getting educational partners involved in committee work. A very important part of making your committee work is being welcoming of participants, but also giving the committee a genuine voice:

> In order to get community involvement, we follow a plan involving 3 things: first of all we **invite** our parents, and our neighbours, and any partner that is willing to come along with us to try to forward our initiatives for safe schools. We also then try to **include** them in whatever discussions there are, in terms of any initiative that is going to happen, any change that is going to happen about the school and anything that affects our community. And finally, we believe, that **influence** is very important. If we invite people in and we ask for their input we believe that they should have some influence on how we manage, how we operate the school. (Principal)

Once your committee has convened, you will want to create with them a vision of a safe, secure, warm and welcoming school. Taking time to develop a vision is necessary to ensure that you and your committee share a sense of direction and will bring energy to your work. A good starting point is to educate your committee members about the current issues that most schools have to confront in the field of safe schools such as bullying and other effects of media violence.

EDUCATING YOUR SAFE SCHOOLS COMMITTEE

How you engage your committee in the process of learning more about safe schools research and findings is extremely important. As mentioned previously, you may want to have each member of the committee start by completing the School Assessment Checklist. Through completing the checklist, committee members will be introduced to the wide variety of factors that influence school safety, including policies and procedures, interventions, violence prevention programs, and school climate. As well, it may assist you to begin to identify areas that need to be addressed.

In order to ensure that the committee members share a common understanding of safe schools challenges, you will need to spend some time in the beginning providing them with information on safe schools. There are many excellent web sites on bullying, violence prevention and media violence to which you may refer the committee members. Local experts are often willing to address such groups for no fee or a minimal cost. There may be particular expertise among the parent body that can be accessed for such professional development. Educating themselves about safe schools will be an ongoing mandate of your committee.

ASSESSING YOUR SCHOOL'S NEEDS AND RESOURCES

Once your committee or team feels comfortable with their knowledge about safe school topics such as bullying and sexual harassment, your safe school team will want to take the time to assess your schools needs through a variety of methods including surveys of students, staff and parents; focus groups, audits of the physical plant, and a review of existing programs and policies. This process is really two-fold—surveys and focus groups serve not only to gather information for the committee, but also to build awareness about school safety and to engage your educational partners in the process.

In order to assess your school climate and establish a baseline before you establish your safe schools goals, your safe schools committee should consider surveying students, staff and parents to gain their perspectives on school safety. Student surveys can answer questions about how safe students feel at school, whether they are bullied, what type of bullying they have experienced, the frequency of bullying, areas of the school where they feel unsafe, homophobia, sexual harassment, and gender violence. Questions should address areas about perpetration and victimization, and also experiences as bystanders. In addition to assessing negative behaviours you may wish to assess positive ones (such as help-seeking) and perceived norms and attitudes. You may also choose to survey parents and/or staff about school climate.

Many administrators may feel overwhelmed at this point when they have a lot of, and possibly contradictory, data. Assistance in analyzing the data you collect may be available through research services at your school board or through community partners with specialized expertise. If you do not have the resources to analyze a large survey, you may want to carefully consider what information you really need and restrict the length of your survey. Conversely, consider using the survey developed by the Canadian Public Health Association (outlined later in this chapter) which offers templates for analysis of your survey. Your survey will provide you with baseline data and may be re-used in the future to track your progress. In exceptional circumstances where research funds and partners are available, these data may become part of a more elaborate study on the effectiveness of the initiatives.

THAMES VALLEY DISTRICT SCHOOL BOARD SURVEY

It is prudent to choose a survey that has been used successfully. There are several excellent surveys readily available. As we mentioned in Chapter 1, the Thames Valley District School Board surveyed all of their students in 2005 and 2006 and have published the results on their web page at www.tvdsb.on.ca/safeschools/. There were two forms of the survey, one for elementary students in grades 4 through 8 and another for secondary students. The elementary survey was divided into 6 sections as follows:

Students were asked to respond to several questions in each section using 5-point Likert scales (e.g., from was a particular school strategy "not very helpful" up to "very helpful"). The students had an opportunity to write their comments at the end of the survey. The secondary school survey was similar but more detailed. Students were asked their perceptions about the school followed by a series of questions on personal safety (where in the school do they feel safe or unsafe), incidents, and then three scenarios asking how the student would respond to given situations. The scenario questions were followed by questions on reporting bullying and dealing with bullying. Students were asked to respond to these questions using a five-point scale from "not very effective" to "very effective". In the final section of the survey, students were asked to respond to a list of strategies to deal with bullying on a five-point scale from "would not really help a lot" to "would really help a lot". High school students were also given an opportunity to make a comment at the end of the survey. The two publications, one for elementary schools and one for secondary, will provide you not only with an excellent survey, but also with the results from the Thames Valley District School Board to which you may compare your own results if such a comparison is meaningful based on the nature of your school and district.

The Thames Valley District School Board followed up on their results by sending individual school results to each school combined with the overall Board results as a basis for comparison. School principals were directed to follow-up by organizing focus groups of all educational partners, including students, parents, support staff, teachers, administrators, and community members. In these sessions, the facilitator shared information with the focus group participants on the data from their own school compared to the overall Board data. As well, the facilitator provided information on the nature and causes of bullying behaviour and its effects on students, those who bully, those who are the victims and the majority who are the bystanders. The School Board provided guidelines on how their survey results could be used to direct discussion of the focus group or safe school committee (see appendix A). This presentation was followed by a brainstorming session involving the use of the fishbone graphic and the format outlined later in this chapter. This example demonstrates how assessment is not solely an information gathering enterprise but can be used to mobilize a system. The TVDSB has used the initial survey as baseline information on school safety and has recently re-surveyed students to monitor progress in their system. They will continue this process by re-assessing the entire student population every five years.

ONTARIO SCHOOL CLIMATE SURVEYS

The Ontario Government had developed School Climate Surveys which are available on the Ministry of Education website at www.edu.gov.on.ca/eng/teachers/climate.html. The Ministry includes surveys covering grades 4 to 12 and for parents and staff on its web site. As well as asking a student's gender and grade, the Ministry school survey asks a student's first language, his/her ability to read and write English and how long that student has lived in Canada. There is an optional question on race, colour of skin or country of origin. The survey begins with a page defining bullying and then asks students questions in the following categories:

At the end of the survey, students are given the opportunity to write comments on school safety. The grades 7 to 12 survey is similar to the elementary survey with additional questions on how teachers and administration at the school respond to bullying, whether or not the code of conduct is enforced, whether or not complaints are acted on and whether or not the student feels the school is taking the appropriate steps to remedy bullying. Again, the students are asked to make any comments on their school's safety. There are 29 items on the secondary school survey compared with 27 items on the elementary school survey. The Ministry emphasizes the use of surveys to provide baseline data on the nature and extent of bullying at the school and for use in reassessment as one indication of the effectiveness of your strategies.

CANADIAN PUBLIC HEALTH ASSOCIATION SURVEY

The Canadian Public Health Association (CPHA) also has an excellent assessment tool available on its website which can be found at the following URL address: http://acsp.cpha.ca/antibullying/english/backinfo/safe_school_study_final.pdf.

In a project funded by the National Crime Prevention Strategy, Department of Public Safety and Emergency Preparedness and in partnership with the Canadian Initiative for the Prevention of Bullying,[27] the CPHA researched and developed this toolkit for schools. In addition to sample surveys, this toolkit includes information on bullying, sexual harassment, and racial discrimination as well as approaches to modifying school climate and best practices. The surveys include sample letters of consent and instructions on how to administer the survey. An excel file for managing the data can be downloaded from the site.

In summary, surveys can be used as a baseline to identify a school's needs as well as a way to measure the effectiveness of your safe school initiatives going forward. You will want to plan to re-survey your school partners on a regular basis.

FOCUS GROUPS

Another valuable method for gathering information about your school is to conduct focus groups with your students, parents, staff and community members. Focus groups offer a number of advantages compared to surveys or individual interviews. They do not have the same

---

[27] The CIPB was a precursor to the PREVNet initiative outlined in Chapter 1. PREVNet continues to work on assessment tools and approaches and is a good resource in this regard.

reading comprehension demands as surveys. Similar to individual interviews you are able to follow up on specific answers and get more detail, but the group format makes it a more efficient process. Individuals may be more comfortable answering questions in a group than one-on-one. There are many guides available for conducting focus groups. At the very least, you may want to consider the following points:

- A written plan is important to maintain focus and ensure that you obtain the desired information. Your plan can either include many specific questions or be more of a content guide from which questions are developed during the focus group.

- It is important to emphasize that a focus group is not a consensus driven process and that you are looking for areas where people have different perspectives.

- Information needs to be recorded as closely as possible in the participants' own words. Facilitators may consider the use of a designated note taker or audio record the session.

It is helpful to have written instructions to guide the facilitators. For example, the following script could be used to begin a focus group with youth. Note that it is advisable to include a reminder about limits to confidentiality:

The staff at this school recognize that students learn best when they are in a safe and caring environment. We are conducting several discussion groups with youth in the hopes that you will share your views on the school climate and relationships among students and adults as openly and honestly as possible. The purpose of this discussion group is not to reach perfect agreement among participants but to better understand and respect different opinions. We may summarize your answers at different points to make sure we understand what you are saying. We hope you will clarify or expand on these answers if you feel we have not heard you correctly.

We are going to ask for your opinion on these issues and we want you to know that although we will be letting staff know your overall opinions, we will not tell them who said what. That will be confidential. If, however, any of you disclose that you've been abused or harassed or if any of you make threats to harm someone else we will not keep that confidential and will need to follow school policies.

We are not experts on this program, so if anything seems unclear we will be asking you to tell us more as we go along.

In addition to providing clear instructions prior to beginning the focus group, it is important to offer some sort of debriefing at the end. At the very least, participants need to know whom they could contact if they are uncomfortable or dissatisfied with the process.

While some facilitators may feel comfortable working from scripts such as these and a set of questions or guidelines, others may prefer a more highly structured approach, such as the one described below.

USING A STRUCTURED FISHBONE APPROACH

One way to structure a focus group is to use a tool such as a "fishbone diagram". As we traveled around the province we used a very simple fishbone graphic to structure our brainstorming exercise. We used the head of the fish to express our goal, "Preventing Violence and Promoting Healthy Relationships". Other goals could be substituted. The Thames Valley District School Board used as its goal "The Prevention of Bullying Behaviour". Your committee should determine the goal for the fishbone exercise. It can be very broad or quite specific depending on your needs. The fishbone and specific instructions for using the fishbone exercise are provided in Figure 1. Each of the fish fins represents partners in education: parents, students, staff and administration, school board, community and other (e.g., the media). The importance of involving all of your partners in education cannot be overemphasized. The focus group activity and the surveys provide excellent opportunities to engage your partners right at the beginning of your safe school needs assessment. The effectiveness of your needs assessment and your future planning depends on the engagement of not only your teaching staff, but also your custodial staff, administrative staff, and other support staff. You should also engage your community partners including the Police Services, Public Health, any local agencies that may be involved in your school, your community representative on your School Council and other interested community partners. Sexual assault and rape crisis centres as well as shelters for abuse victims can add important expertise on gender-based violence. Students, themselves, can be a powerful ally in safe schools planning. In fact, most students indicate that they feel quite strongly that they should be involved in the solution to violence in their school. As we traveled across the province, students as young as those in grade 3 offered insightful solutions to addressing violence in schools. To be an effective method of information gathering, it is important to have as many people as possible at the table for your fishbone brainstorming sessions. However, there are several ways of organizing your focus groups and these should be considered carefully.

You may want to run a large session with several partners sitting at different tables at a time when most of your partners are available such as over the lunch hour or in the evening. You will need to decide how you want to organize your working groups. You may chose to have a mixture of partners such as staff, students, parents, community members at each table or you may chose more homogenous groupings with students at one table, staff at another, etc. This will be an important decision for your committee as it will have an effect on the results. You will have to decide if your students will be more reticent in a mixed group including parents leading you to prefer homogenous groups. If you feel that the cross-fertilization of ideas is more important, you may prefer to organize your brainstorming session into mixed groups. Heterogeneous groups offer the significant advantage of having the various partners hear differing perceptions about school safety. The focus group can make teachers more aware of parents' perceptions and parents more aware of some of the efforts the staff is undertaking to make the school safe.

Rather than organize one large session, another approach is to organize multiple focus groups at different times to capture as many people as possible. You may want to do a brainstorming session with the whole staff present, for example. You may choose to work with students on a separate occasion and the parents and community at an evening event. In this case, your analysis of the data from the brainstorming sessions may reveal a difference in perception among the groups. While staff may feel that much more work needs to be done, students may send the message that much is being done and that they feel quite safe. The reverse may emerge where the staff feels that the school is doing an excellent job in preventing bullying and promoting healthy relationships, but students or parents may have different perceptions. In any case, it is important to have a mix of educational partners participate in the process. Often the most effective events occur when all partners are in the room. Even if you choose to conduct focus groups with homogenous groups, such as students, or if you do not choose to hold one large session with many partners in attendance, information should be shared with all groups in a whole group debriefing or at some other point.

AUDITS OF PHYSICAL PLANT

Another important aspect of your safe schools needs assessment is an audit of your physical plant, including both the interior of the school and the exterior and grounds. In 2005, the Province of Ontario conducted an audit of the physical plant of every school in Ontario. We have taken the audit form used by the Province and have revised it to include only items relating to issues of safety from the point of view of physical plant issues. It is included on page 73. You may modify this for your specific needs, but it provides a good template for the items that need to be considered. An audit of your physical plant is a great starting point for a Stage 1 school as all partners understand safety in this basic physical sense. However, it is important to educate partners to think about safety in a more comprehensive sense and not allow a physical plant audit to serve as an overall school safety assessment.

It is important to involve your custodial staff and possibly someone from police services in the safety audit of the building and grounds. You and your committee will want to assign individuals to walk around the school and look for areas of the school which are not easily visible to staff and administration, where there is poor lighting, and where incidents occur frequently. Each auditor should have a section of the checklist to complete. Having two or three people work on each section of the survey will ensure that there are more eyes and ears to observe any safety concerns.

You will also want to review the playground and look for areas of potential danger, such as bushes that hide sight-lines, equipment that may cause injury because it is poorly maintained, and proximity to parking lots and roads. Details of emergency response procedures and plans may also be reviewed as part of your audit of your facility in order to provide more information than the School Assessment Checklist in the area of policies and procedures. If in reviewing the results of your School Assessment Checklist, you find that you have work to be done in the area of policies and procedures, the information from the Safety Audit will provide more detailed ideas about how to get started. Finally, you will want to examine whether or not your school's access is well signed and secure.

UNDERSTANDING THE DATA

Once your safe school committee has completed its investigation of your school's needs, it is time to do some planning on how to address the identified areas of needs. It is advisable to involve the whole committee in setting goals and planning. Your first step will involve a careful analysis and overview of the data you have received from the survey results, focus groups and audit of the physical plant. From these data, you will be able to identify areas in the schools, or specific times when students feel unsafe. You may have identified that incidents of bullying in the school are higher than you thought and you may have new information on the type of bullying that is most prevalent. You may have identified unsafe areas in your school where additional lighting or increased supervision is needed. Perhaps there is a need to improve the consistency of responses to incidents of violent behaviour. All of this information will assist you to identify strategies and programs that you will need to make your school safer. However, you will need to take time to fully understand the data that you have gathered and to establish priorities for action. Creating a safe school is a complex and multidimensional undertaking, so it is not simply a matter of generating an overall score. Rather, it is akin to developing a profile of strengths and problem areas to guide next steps.

Now that you have your data it may be tempting to launch a rapid response in areas that you perceive to be problematic. Additionally, you may experience external pressure from parents and the larger community to "deal with" any newly identified problems. In some situations this pressure may be exacerbated by a recent critical incident. In other circumstances there may be a parent or a teacher who wants to replicate a model program operating well in a neighbouring school.

In any event, you will be better served by having a systematic plan for approaching your data rather than by succumbing to pressure for an immediate solution. It is useful to reference a set of guidelines for interpreting data, such as those developed by the Thames Valley District School Board to assist administrators in understanding their school profiles (see Appendix 1).

Some of these guidelines and additional suggestions from our team include:

- Compare individual school results with the full board results (where available) to identify differences and to consider what might account for those differences.
- Consider the context of your school, including demographic characteristics, what proportion of students are transported by bus, the mobility of the student population and any other factors that might have affected the results.
- Look at the size and type of your play yard, the design of the school building and the school surroundings when interpreting your data. Is your school located at a busy intersection or on a quiet street? Is there a mall or retail strip nearby? These details will provide an important context in regards to staff supervision and students' perceptions of external threats to safety.
- Be careful about interpreting results if the school has a small population. In that case, relatively few students may have a large impact on the results in percentage terms.
- Consider all the data. If you have conducted focus groups and completed the School Assessment Checklist, this information needs to be considered in light of the survey results. What are the areas of agreement? If there are significant differences, is further inquiry required?
- Use the results of your survey, focus groups and School Assessment Checklist as a springboard for discussion and dialogue.

ESTABLISHING PRIORITIES

Following your discussion of the results of your information gathering, you and your safe schools committee will want to look at data in a little more detail and reach a consensus on which areas need to be addressed first. In other words, take some time to establish your priorities. You will find that the School Assessment Checklist will be helpful in describing your school's stage of change in the four major areas: policies and procedures, interventions, prevention and school climate. Clearly, if you have identified that you are in Stage 1 or early Stage 2 in any of these areas, you will want to address that consideration first. The School Assessment Checklist is an excellent vehicle for identifying areas that need your attention.

After establishing short and medium-term priorities, you can turn your attention to setting some specific and measurable goals for the school year. Specific and measurable goals are better than vague statements because they allow progress to be tracked more accurately. For example, "increasing the number of parents on your safe schools committee to four" is a better goal than "increasing parent involvement" because you will be able to assess your progress clearly. The goals that you set will need to be reviewed at the end of the year and, based on your findings, will need to be revised and renewed. Your annual review should be built into your plans.

SUMMARY

Once you have gathered together and analyzed all of your information, you will be ready to move to the planning stage, as outlined in the following chapter. Using a variety of assessment tools you have identified which stage of change best describes your school's safety in four major areas: policies and procedures, intervention, prevention, and school climate. From that information, you and your committee can begin to develop specific goals for your safe school agenda for the coming year. Matching these goals to the stage of change for your school will build a foundation for sustainability of these strategies in years to come.

Sustainable Strategies For Safe Schools
School Consultations

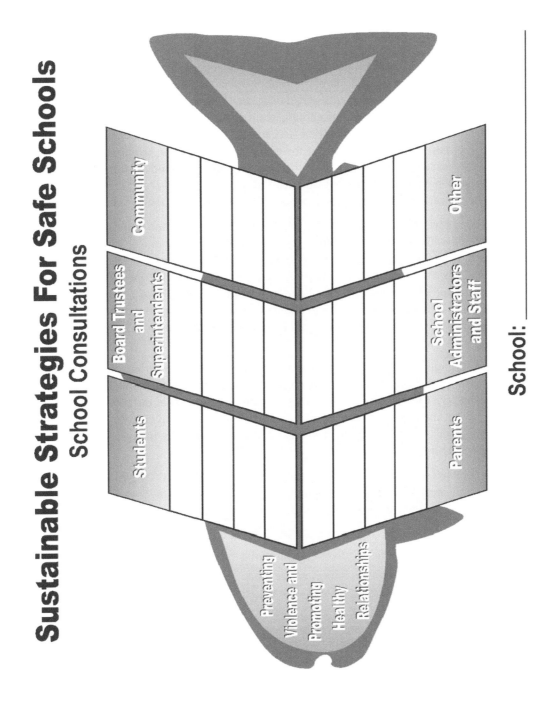

School:

Instructions:

1. Participants will work at tables in groups of 4 or 5. Generally, there will be a mix of representation at the table (e.g., teacher, parent, etc.). However, this exercise may be done with one group only, for example, staff members on a professional development day, or students, or parents at a school council meeting. The number and size of the working groups will be determined by the registration of participants.

2. The head of the fishbone, "Preventing Violence and Promoting Healthy Relationships", is the focus of the discussion. The titles on the outside of the fishbone provide the reference points for brainstorming. For example, participants would be asked to discuss, the role community partners could play in preventing violence and promoting healthy relationships. One possible response would be public health nurses provide presentations to parents, students and school staff on related topics. As each group brainstorms, the recorder for the group writes down the key points on the line from the spine to the box. Once the group has finished with one box, they move on to the next box. For example, "What can peers do to prevent violence and promote healthy relationships?" Depending on the number of participants, each group will be asked to complete one or two specific boxes.

3. Once the groups have completed their "fins", the recorders will be asked to move to the next table to share their ideas. Generally, it is helpful if each recorder is asked to move clockwise to the next table. Each recorder then explains to the new group the ideas that were recorded and asks the new group to make any additions. Then the recorder should be requested to move to the next table to repeat the process. This "walkabout" is particularly helpful when you have groups working on only one or two fins since it gives participants an opportunity to share ideas that relate to other partners in education. Once two other tables have been visited, the recorder should return to his original group.

4. When the "walkabout" is completed and new entries added, the recorder may share any additional ideas with his original group. At this point each group is asked to use the highlighters on their tables in the following way: they will use a blue marker to highlight things that the group feels are in place—things their school and community have well underway in terms of implementation. They will use yellow for things which are in progress or in the initial stages and leave the rest of the items un-coloured indicating they need improvement.

5. Once this is completed, the group will be instructed to circle ONE or TWO items which they feel their school community needs to focus on developing further, in other words, priorities for action. The group should consider next steps and what they need to make this happen.

6. The facilitator will ask each group to present their items and would record the results on an overhead projector.

7. The facilitator will ask the group the following question: "Given all your assets that you are proud of, what are three things that you don't have now that could move this process forward?"

School Policies/Procedures

Access & Visitors	Yes	No	NA
During school hours, visitors can only access our school through one clearly marked door.			
Students, visitors and staff are welcomed as they enter the school.			
We have signs that request that all visitors check in to the office.			
Directions to our main office are clearly displayed.			
We have a visitor sign-in policy.			
Our visitors must wear a visitor badge/nametag.			

Attendance/Absence	Yes	No	NA
Our students need written permission to leave school during school hours. *(Elementary schools only)*			
Our students must be picked up by a parent or individual with written permission and proper identification and there is a process that ensures that this is the case. *(Elementary Schools Only)*			
Parents are notified if students are absent from class.			

In-school Communication	Yes	No	NA
We have portable communications devices (e.g., two-way radios, cell phones).			
Using the comments section please identify who uses the portable communication devices and why?			
We have two-way communication between our main office and classrooms, portables.			
We have a central alarm/emergency system in the building and portables.			

Emergency Response	Yes	No	NA
We have an emergency preparedness plan.			
Our staff have been assigned responsibilities for different parts of the emergency plans.			
We have a lock-down/evacuation plan.			
We have a plan to deal with the aftermath of a violent incident.			
We have established an emergency control centre and evacuation sites.			
Our students' information is available in case of emergency.			
We have police protocols in place.			
We do maintenance and/or testing of the entire security system at least every six months.			
We have emergency kits (e.g. megaphone and flashlights).			
We have a first aid kit.			
Our staff are trained in first aid and CPR.			

	Yes	No	NA
Monitoring			
Our staff supervise the student pick-up/drop-off zone. (*Elementary schools only*)			
Our staff monitor/supervise school grounds before/after school, recess and lunch. (*Elementary schools only*)			
All staff members are required to lock classrooms upon leaving.			
Our students are restricted from entering unused classrooms alone.			
Restrooms are regularly monitored by staff.			
Our staff are assigned responsibilities for monitoring/supervising students outside the classroom (i.e., hallways, cafeteria/lunch areas, etc.).			
Staff/adult supervision is present when the gym is in use by students.			
Our students are supervised while loitering in corridors, hallways, stairwells and restrooms. (*Secondary Schools Only*)			
A person is designated to perform a comprehensive security check at the end of the day.			
We have a Safe Arrivals program. (*Elementary schools only*)			
Physical Structure			
Lighting	Yes	No	NA
Our buildings and portables are well lit.			
Our grounds are well lit.			
Our hallways and stairwells are well lit.			
Our restrooms are well lit.			
Access & Security	Yes	No	NA
Window locks are functional.			
Window/basement windows are protected (e.g., grill or well covers).			
Portables are visible from the main building.			
Main entrance/lobby to school property can be observed from the school office.			
Security and access devices are in place at the school to monitor the main entrance if not visible from the school office.			
Security/surveillance cameras are in place at the school. (If yes, please use comment section to describe how many and where.)			
We can close unused areas of school after school hours.			
In emergency situation, staff, students and visitors can exit the school safely.			
Grounds	Yes	No	NA
Our JK/SK play areas are fenced. (*Elementary Schools Only*)			
Shrubs and foliage are trimmed to allow for good line of sight.			
All of our school buildings and grounds are accessible to security and emergency vehicles.			
Snow mounds are positioned to minimize obstruction of portables and school grounds.			
Our school's exterior walls are free from graffiti.			
Have there been broken windows/incidents of graffiti experienced in our school in the past 3 months?			
Have there been any break-ins into our schools or portables during the past year?			

	Yes	No	NA
Are police advised of break-ins and major incidents of vandalism?			
Has there been ongoing vandalism?			
(Answer only if you answered yes to the previous question.) In light of the ongoing vandalism, has the Principal requested special attention (proactive security patrols) from Board Security or local police?			
Is there an area with easy roof access?			
Our school's grounds are free from trash or debris.			
Student access to parking area is restricted to arrival and dismissal times. **(Elementary Schools Only)**			
Is visitor parking available and well marked?			
Is visitor parking in an area that can be observed from the main office or other staffed areas?			
Secure Areas	**Yes**	**No**	**NA**
Is school property engraved with police provided ID code?			
Does our school staff deposit cash funds on a regular basis?			
Are cash funds kept in a secure central area?			

> *If a man knows not what harbor he seeks,*
> *any wind is the right wind.*
> *-Seneca*

Now that you have a clear sense of your school's profile in the four areas—policies and procedures, intervention, prevention and school climate—you can begin to choose specific strategies to move your school towards sustainable action. The advantage of a stage-based model of change is that you increase your likelihood of success by matching strategies and programs to your school's stage. Depending on your school's stage in each area, there is a wide range of strategies that you may want to consider. The overview of which strategies match the individual stages is outlined in Appendix 2. In the following sections this process is explained in more detail for each stage.

YOUR SCHOOL IS IN STAGE 1

Typically, the activities associated with making progress in a Stage 1 school include naming and describing the problem, examining, surveying, and investigating. If you have followed the procedures outlined in Chapters 4 and 5, you will already be familiar with many of these Stage 1 activities. Data gathering and auditing are extremely important basic activities to complete in order to move your school forward. In a Stage 1 school you may want to prioritize continuing activities to raise awareness of the need for violence prevention and to promote healthy relationships. Some activities that you may consider to raise awareness include:

- Organizing assemblies featuring motivational speakers on safe school topics such as bullying, racism, homophobia, harassment, media violence, and cyber bullying. When you are arranging to have motivational speakers speak to the entire school body in an assembly, it is important to plan and provide for follow-up debriefing activities when the students return to their classrooms following such a presentation.
- Screening videos that address these issues. One such video that is available from the Thames Valley District School Board was produced by secondary school students for their peers. The

video, *Angel*, deals with bullying in a secondary school situation and provides an excellent opportunity to observe the positive and negative effects of bystanders who observe the bullying behaviour. This video is particularly suitable for showing in individual classrooms and includes some debriefing discussion pointers for teachers to use. One of our participating schools uses this video effectively every fall term with their grade 9 classes. The advantage of showing this video in class is that there is an opportunity for discussion and debriefing immediately following the video.

- Presenting live theatre dealing with social issues to the students. In Toronto, Trinity Theatre provides theatrical productions for students that focus on social relationships. In other communities and schools, a Forum Theatre may be presented. Forum Theatre is an interactive approach that involves the audience in developing real-time strategies for dealing with social and personal issues.

- Engaging parents through offering parent education in the evenings on cyber bullying, media violence, harassment and other safe schools topics. Particular efforts will be required to engage parents, especially in a Stage 1 school.

- Using the school newsletter and/or school website to inform parents of safe school activities at your school and to educate them about various safe school issues. Many schools include links to web sites that will assist parents to deal with bullying, harassment, homophobia, media violence, and cyber bullying. At one of our participating schools, the Youth Safe Schools Committee posted myths of bullying on their website and a quiz about alcohol and drugs for students and/or parents to complete.

POLICIES AND PROCEDURES

While the above-listed activities provide strategies to raise general awareness of violence prevention in your school, you may want to specifically address one or more of the four specific domains within your school. For example, if you have identified that your school is in Stage 1 in policies and procedures, you will first want to review your emergency procedures, safe school arrival policy, and Code of Conduct to ensure that they reflect current provincial and board policies. This audit may be done with your safe school committee, a committee of administration and staff or with an ad hoc committee of staff, students and parents. As part of your policy and procedure review, you and your committee could undertake the following:

- ☑ Audit your school's Code of Conduct, Mission Statement and Vision for inclusive language and compatibility with the Safe Schools provincial legislation and consistency with your School Board's policies
- ☑ Audit how consistently the Code of Conduct is enforced by staff and school administration. This audit could be done with some short surveys of students and staff or independent observations.

☑ Review procedures for handling harassment complaints and harassment incidents.
☑ Review your lock down procedures on at least an annual basis (e.g., Are they understood, posted, practised? Are the emergency preparedness plans in place)?
☑ Survey classroom rules used in the school for the use of inclusive language.
☑ Assess how well staff and students know the protocols and policies around issues of bullying, harassment, Code of Conduct infractions.

Most school boards have sample school-based policies that you may use as a starting point to revise your current policies. It is important that once you have revised your policies and interventions you communicate the revised policies to your educational partners and to provide in-service for your staff on their implementation. These implementation pieces are essentially Stage 2 activities, and will be discussed further in that section.

INTERVENTION

If your data indicate that your intervention strategies are in Stage 1, then you will want to review your reporting and intervention procedures with both students and staff. At this stage, you and your safe schools committee will want to increase awareness among all stakeholders about the need for appropriate intervention. You will want to investigate ways for all stakeholders to report and appropriately respond to incidents of violence. The areas that you should include in your audit of intervention strategies might include the following:

- Do students who observe bullying behaviour know how to respond appropriately?
- Are students reporting incidents of bullying or violent behaviour to staff and administration?
- Do you have protocols in place to allow students to anonymously report incidents of bullying behaviour? Are procedures in place that ensure confidentiality of this information? Do the students feel comfortable reporting incidents and knowing that their safety is ensured?
- Does the staff feel comfortable intervening in an incident of bullying or violent behaviour?
- Does the staff know and follow procedures for reporting incidents of bullying or violent behaviour to the administration?
- Is there a follow-up procedure in place that supports both the bully and the victim?
- Do your intervention protocols allow you to appropriately recognize and respond to the uniqueness of each situation?
- How consistently are protocols and procedures applied by staff?
- Have all of your staff, both teaching and non-teaching, received training on how to recognize and de-escalate potentially violent situations?

If you have identified that your school is in Stage 1 in the area of prevention, you will want to review your prevention programming throughout the school. At this stage, you and your committee need to spend some time reviewing the programs that are available. You may choose to focus on bullying, character education or both, depending on the results of your survey and personal philosophy. Some educators prefer to focus on Character Education because of the positive connotation, but it is important that you also give the students the tools to understand and respond appropriately to bullying behaviour.

Educators in our study described a sense of being overwhelmed with the number of prevention programs available. Some principals report being bombarded with glossy flyers, emails, and phone solicitation promising innovative programs to address bullying and harassment. Overall, they expressed a need to sort through the merits of individual programs and the extent to which they match the stage and resources available for their school. In sorting through the various options available, it may be helpful to consider how the programs are different. RESOLVE Alberta[28] has published a compendium of available prevention programs, and include a useful framework for understanding the differences among them. Although more information is available from the RESOLVE website, we highlight the dimensions for consideration here:

- Qualifications of Program Staff – what are the qualifications and training of the implementers?
- Presentation Format – is there sufficient duration and follow-up?
- Curriculum – coverage of topics and alignment with ministry objectives
- Reaction to Program – including dealing with disclosures
- Evaluation – extent, form and results of existing evaluations
- Coordination of Efforts – does the program have a role for multiple stakeholders?
- Cost of Program – both direct and indirect
- Availability – is there a waitlist?
- Policy and procedure – does it align with your school and board policies?

---

[28] RESOLVE Alberta's manual, *School-based violence prevention programs, A resource manual* is available online or for order at http://www.ucalgary.ca/resolve/violenceprevention/English/index.htm

The aforementioned RESOLVE website documents a wide variety of available programs with an analysis on the dimensions listed.

SCHOOL CLIMATE

In many schools that we visited, the principals chose to focus first on establishing a school climate that was warm and welcoming and embracing of diversity. A positive school climate is characterized by personal relationships, modeled within a school, that demonstrate mutual acceptance, inclusion and respect. If you have identified that your school is in Stage 1 in school climate, you may want to undertake the following:

- ☑ Develop an awareness of how inclusive language is used in the classroom and in student assignments (e.g., family tree assignments, role models, historical figures, and hero assignments).
- ☑ Examine how question-friendly the classroom is (e.g., do we work at establishing an environment where it is acceptable for students to ask questions about what we don't understand with respect to diversity of race, creed, colour, disability, and other individual differences).
- ☑ Survey classroom rules used in the school for the use of inclusive language.
- ☑ Determine the extent of involvement of your educational partners in school activities and safe school programs.
- ☑ Assess how welcoming your school is for students. Are the halls bright and cheerfully decorated? Are students valued and encouraged? Do students feel safe and secure in your school?
- ☑ Consider whether student diversity reflected in the posters and other material is present in the school?

During our research we were able to identify several schools that were in an overall Stage 1. One of these, Northwest Secondary School, was introduced on page 39. In the following text box, the recommendations that emerged for Northwest, based on the assessment process, are outlined. Note that all but one of the recommendations focuses on assemblies, newsletter articles, parents' evenings and surveys in order to raise awareness of the need to prevent violence and promote healthy relationships.

- Focus on increasing awareness of staff, students and parents about bullying behaviour and other safe school-related issues through assemblies for students that included a follow-up in the classroom
- Provide staff training in identifying and responding to bullying behaviour
- Publish articles on safe schools in the school newsletter
- Provide parent evenings on safe school issues such as media violence, cyber bullying and violence prevention
- Survey students in one class at each grade level and conduct focus groups to further assess the school's needs before developing a safe schools plan.

After sharing these recommendations with the school, the administrator and safe schools team worked to operationalize them as specific and measureable goals against which progress could be tracked.

YOUR SCHOOL IS IN STAGE 2

Some of the activities associated with making progress in a Stage 2 school include engaging, implementing, reinforcing, training, and developing action plans, and working to involve all stakeholders. Stage 2 is the stage where you will need to refine and implement your safe school plans. As with Stage 1, there may be some variability in your progress across different areas, in which case it will be important to make plans for each area as described below.

POLICIES AND PROCEDURES

If your school is in Stage 2 with respect to policies and procedures, you need to concentrate on further developing and communicating your emergency procedures to all stakeholders and training staff on an ongoing basis to implement policies and procedures consistently. Your committee may find that all of your policies and procedures reflect current best practices and are appropriate for your school community. In that case, you may consider that it is not the content of the policies and procedures that is lacking rather widespread awareness and enforcement of these policies. If it is the awareness and enforcement that are weak, you may want to:

- ☑ Raise the profile of your Code of Conduct by ensuring that every school partner has read and understood it. Some of our schools sent a copy of the Code of Conduct home every fall and required that parents sign that they have read and acknowledge it. This review was also done in classrooms where students were requested to sign that they have read and will comply with the school's rules.
- ☑ Review the extent to which protocols for crisis intervention balance adhering to set principles with recognizing the uniqueness of a particular situation.
- ☑ Choose to develop a secure, safe anonymous reporting system so that students can report incidents in the knowledge that their report will be kept confidential and their safety will be ensured.
- ☑ Communicate, plan and practise the lock down procedures, tornado drills, fire drills and safe evacuations of the school.
- ☑ Provide professional development for your staff to ensure that they are aware of and know how to enforce student policies. The staff needs to be clear about progressive discipline procedures, how to keep records and when to refer incidents to the office.
- ☑ Train staff at all levels on how to recognize and de-escalate potentially volatile student situations.

INTERVENTION

If you are in Stage 2 in the area of intervention, you will continue to engage your school partners in understanding the problem and making the links between violence and gender, race or vulnerabilities so that your educational partners can be more empathetic and more in tune with students' realities. The better your partners understand the complex nature of violence and harassment, the easier it will be to elicit the appropriate response to various situations that might arise. In the case of intervention, some of the programs associated with this stage include teaching appropriate bystander behaviour, developing appropriate interventions, teaching students peer mediation techniques and training staff to respond to incidents of violence appropriately and with confidence.

An important aspect of intervention for a Stage 2 school is to ensure engagement of all the partners as comprehensively as possible. A good example of this principle is to engage all students as part of the solution for a violence-free community. Interventions cannot focus exclusively on victims and perpetrators, but have to consider the critical role of students as bystanders and peer helpers. You need to communicate this principle to all students so they can recognize their own responsibilities as bystanders, even if they are silent. Bystander intervention in incidents of bullying is a very effective intervention, and research has shown that when peers speak up against bullying, they successfully end the incident more than half the time.[29] PREVnet has easily downloadable "Tip Sheets", available on its web site at www.prevnet.ca, that are appropriate for both elementary and secondary schools that outline appropriate responses for "bystanders".

Beyond their role as bystanders, students are an underutilized resource as peer mediators and mentors. Whether you choose the whole school approach and teach all students how to act as peer mediators, or whether you select a cadre of responsible and well-trained senior students to act as peer mediators, this can be an effective approach to involve student bystanders in solving conflicts in the school. Few of the schools that we visited actually had an active peer mediation program up and running. This may be a reflection of the time and commitment required of staff and students to maintain an effective peer mediation program.

Although we have focused on the role of students as allies in responding to incidents of violence, staff members are obviously a key component in a comprehensive plan. Everything staff members do and say in a school provides a message to students. Learning opportunities go well beyond the curriculum and happen in the daily teachable moments in hallways, eating areas, and gymnasiums. The staff needs to be engaged with the safe schools agenda, feel confident in their ability to respond to student behaviour, and share ownership of the issue. In several of our participating schools the principals reported that the following discussions were features of each and every staff meeting:

- ☑ Responding to bullying behaviour;
- ☑ Documenting progressive discipline procedures and detailing what happens when a student is referred to the office;
- ☑ Developing a consistent response on the part of staff.

---

[29] Craig, W. & Pepler, D. (1997). *How peers influence bullying.* Available at www.prevnet.ca

In Stage 2 of intervention, the focus is on ensuring that your staff has the tools and the motivation to respond to bullying situations and other misdemeanors appropriately. While your staff may now be fully aware of the need for appropriate responses, they will need ongoing training on how to respond to incidents of bullying behaviour and other conflict situations. Research shows that teachers are generally unaware of the extent of bullying problems within their school.[30] Observational data indicate that teachers intervene in 14% of classroom episodes and only 4% of playground episodes of bullying, although teachers estimate their intervention rates as being much higher. Pepler and Craig suggest that low teacher intervention may occur for a number of reasons: the majority of bullying episodes are verbal (and may be missed), episodes are brief, children engaging in bullying have strategies to avoid detection, and bullying tends to occur when monitoring is low.

In many cases awareness that a student is bullying or is being bullied will be through the report of the victim or a bystander. It is critical that the teachers know how to respond appropriately without putting the victim in further jeopardy. Otherwise, the blame for reporting may fall on the victim and there will be possible retribution on the part of the bully. Your staff needs to be aware of this and know how to respond and initiate appropriate administrative involvement.

PREVENTION

Some of the activities that characterize Stage 2 in prevention will include the implementation of bullying prevention programs, character education and other comprehensive age appropriate programs and activities to prevent violence and promote healthy relationships. By this point in time, you have researched and analyzed your school's programming needs and done the research to select the appropriate program for your school. You will be involved in providing the resources, training your staff and beginning to implement your violence prevention program school wide. Actual implementation is discussed in detail in Chapter 7.

---

[30] Pepler, D., Craig, W. (2000). *Making a difference in bullying.* Available at the following website http://www.arts.yorku.ca/lamarsh/pdf/Making_a_Difference_in_Bullying.pdf.

In addition to adult-led programming, some of our schools had effective peer mentoring programs that involved senior students. Sometimes these programs were run entirely outside of the classroom and in other cases students were enrolled in peer mentoring and leadership courses to learn skills of mentoring younger students. These students usually visited grade 9 classes during their homeroom period to discuss social issues with the students and to assist them to know the school better. Generally, they were not involved in mediating conflicts. The Thames Valley District School Board has an innovative peer mentoring program designed specifically to meet the unique strengths and challenges of Aboriginal youth. Pairs or groups of students meet at lunch to engage in a variety of activities with a focus on building healthy relationships. This program also includes adult community mentors who come into the school periodically to provide support to the students, serve as role models, and increase connection to the community. More information about this program is available at www.youthrelationships.org.

SCHOOL CLIMATE

Depending on the developmental stage of your students, you may consider some of the following Stage 2 strategies:

- ☑ Developing a common language of respect within the school through the use of a student pledge that is prominently displayed in the halls and is repeated regularly in daily exercises. There are many examples of pledges of respect available on the internet. However, the process of writing your own pledge in consultation with staff, students and parents is the most effective way of developing a pledge that has meaning for your school. In one of our elementary schools the students repeated their pledge of respect every morning.
- ☑ Holding regular clean-up days and rallies to develop school spirit and a sense of caring for and pride in your school. Taking this idea one step further, one school in our study, organized each class to take responsibility throughout the year for maintaining designated areas of the school or the yard.
- ☑ Establishing student clubs that promote equity, social justice and respect. In one of our schools, the respect club organized activities to celebrate the diverse cultures represented in the school. In another school, the students in the equity club organized a "pink" shirt day to celebrate standing up against harassment and bullying.
- ☑ Introducing an expectation of the use of inclusive, respectful language by all staff, students and parents.

The majority of schools in our study fell predominantly in Stage 2. In Chapter 4 we discussed Riverside Elementary School as an example of a Stage 2 school (page 41). In this particular school, there was a range of progress across the different areas. They had an award system in place, but they had not yet established a viable safe school committee that represented all stakeholders. The following text box outlines the recommendations for Riverside in all areas of its development of its safe schools programming.

> **Recommendations for Riverside Elementary School**
>
> - Review and redevelop the current award system to recognize positive student contributions to creating a safe school environment and give it a high profile within the school and community.
> - Implement a school-wide bullying prevention program.
> - Expand the staff and administrative safe schools committee to include representatives from all support staff groups, parents, senior students and community members.
> - Hold regular meetings of the safe schools committee (three times a year) to review and evaluate all aspects of school safety and to ensure sustainability of all safe school programs.

Within these recommendations, the school was responsible for generating specific goals and indicators of success.

YOUR SCHOOL IS IN STAGE 3

If you have identified that your school is in Stage 3 in one or more of the four identified areas of activity, you and your school should be congratulated! In fact, recognition and celebration is one of the hallmark activities of a Stage 3 school. At the same time, you need to be vigilant and have in place a continuing approach to review, re-evaluation and renewal to ensure that your school continues as a model safe school. Each year, new students, staff and parents will come through your school doors, requiring a system of mentoring and renewal to maintain your success. Some of the activities that you will engage in as a Stage 3 school include consolidating, leading, enhancing, and celebrating. You are comfortable with all of your educational partners at the table. You are willing to share your collective expertise with other schools and jurisdictions.

POLICIES AND PROCEDURES

Most of the policies and procedures at a Stage Three school are embedded into the school's daily routines and meet provincial and board expectations. There is evidence that these policies are being respected and enforced and that there is a positive feeling and pride that your educational partners respect the rules of discipline that are in effect at your school. You have an ongoing plan to share policies with new parents and students to ensure that the entire school community is aware of these guidelines. Reviews of your policies and procedures must occur regularly in order to ensure that you continue to meet expectations from your board and the Ministry of Education. In addition, there are always emerging issues that require new policies. For example, five years ago cyber-bullying was barely on the radar of most educators and now there is a need for clear policies and procedures. A school that is in Stage 3 in any or all of the areas has an ongoing challenge to maintain this level of achievement.

INTERVENTION

Intervention strategies need to be constantly reviewed and updated. Even in a Stage 3 school, the issue of consistency of intervention and appropriate response needs to be an ongoing item on the agenda of staff meetings. While you are now in a position to share your strategies for interventions with other schools and school districts, you must continue to be open to new ideas and to changes. Most schools in Stage 3 have implemented a mentorship program for staff as well as students. These mentoring strategies support continuity in all areas of the school. In particular, these may help ensure that new staff members are aware of your school's safe school policies and procedures and interventions.

PREVENTION

If your school is in Stage 3 in prevention programming, then your programs are already embedded into the curriculum and meet provincial expectations. An important component of maintaining a Stage 3 school is to have a plan for ongoing training for your individual programs. New teachers will need to be trained in existing initiatives, but even those who have already been trained will benefit from ongoing training. Without this ongoing training, the most innovative features of programs (particularly those that involve role play) are likely to be dropped.

One example of an integrated program is the *Fourth R.* Initially developed as a grade 9 physical and health education unit on healthy living that meets the curriculum guidelines of the Province of Ontario, *The Fourth R* has been expanded to include a grade 8 physical and health education program, as well as English programming for grades 9 to 12. The *Fourth R* curricula focus on weaving healthy relationships through all of the programs and developing relationship and critical literacy skills. In all of these programs, care has been taken to ensure that the criteria outlined in the curriculum guidelines are met so that teachers can deliver the curriculum. Furthermore, there is a standardized training for teachers to ensure that they have the necessary information and skills to implement the program. The *Fourth R* has been used in more than 800 schools across the country and also has specialized versions for particular populations and settings[31] (see www.youthrelationships.org).

It is important to celebrate your successes on a regular basis by recognizing students who demonstrate appropriate leadership in violence prevention. One of the schools in our study has a procedure for staff to nominate students to receive a certificate for good citizenship. The staff selects students who have demonstrated caring for their peers, their school, or their environment through their actions. Staff recognition is also extremely important. Whether it is at staff meetings or at full school assembly, your staff members who make a commitment and provide leadership in the area of violence prevention and promoting healthy relationships should be recognized and honoured for their contribution.

Important, as well, is the school's ongoing commitment to reviewing and revising their violence prevention programs. A school that is at Stage 3 should be very comfortable with frank discussions by all school partners on the status of their safe schools programming. Crises will still arise in a Stage 3 school. No one is immune to having some incidents of violence. However, these incidents will happen less often and will be dealt with the most appropriate course of

---

[31] Crooks, C.V., Wolfe, D.A., Hughes, R., Jaffe, P.G., Chiodo, D. (2008). Development, evaluation, and national implementation of a school-based program to reduce violence and related risk behaviours: Lessons from the Fourth R. *Institute for the Prevention of Crime Review, 2,* 109-135.

action. There is no need to cover up when your school is already doing all it can to prevent violence and promote healthy relationships.

SCHOOL CLIMATE

As a Stage 3 school, your school's climate is healthy. Inclusiveness is in evidence everywhere: in school clubs, in the language used by staff and students in school and at events held outside of school. Students and staff feel welcome at your school. Anti-hate clubs, social justice clubs, Gay Lesbian Bisexual Transgendered (GLBT) clubs and alliances are active and well-accepted in your school. Multicultural celebrations are regular occurrences and are enjoyed by the entire student body. In Stage 3 schools, the ownership for safety is shared among adults and youth. Youth might be involved through active safe schools committees that raise awareness, plan events, and celebrate successes.[32]

Only a couple of the schools in our sample were far enough along in their safe schools programming to be considered Stage 3 schools. Lakeview Elementary School (highlighted on page 43) was one such school. This particular school had developed an excellent student leadership program, but numbers involved with the program had been declining. It was decided that more focus needed to be placed on this program to raise its profile within the school. As well, the turnout of parents and community representatives continued to be a challenge for this Stage 3 school. They needed to focus some attention on trying to get more parents and community members involved on their safe schools action team. Finally, this school needed to share its strategies more widely with schools in their jurisdiction. This, in itself, is a way of celebrating their success.

---

[32]A manual for the planning, recruitment, activities, evaluation and succession planning involved with sustaining an active student committee are addressed in a *Fourth R* manual. More information is available at www.youthrelationships.org.

The following recommendations were developed to more firmly establish Lakeview in Stage 3 on the Safe Schools Continuum:

Recommendations for Lakeview Elementary School

- Develop a higher profile for positive student leadership in the school
- Continue to encourage parents and community representatives to have more input into violence prevention policy/leadership groups
- Promote and share programs and strategies with the local community and other schools in the District School Board.

SUMMARY

If you have carefully surveyed, audited, and analyzed your results, you will find that identifying priorities and establishing goals is a challenge, but one that can be met when you have a team of dedicated educational partners working together. In the next chapter, we will look at putting all the pieces together for a successful implementation. We will also identify some of the challenges you may face and provide examples of how approaching these challenges in a systematic way can turn them into opportunities.

Change is a journey – not a blueprint. (Fullan & Miles, 1992)

The preceding chapters in this book have helped you build a vision and an action plan with respect to safe schools. In this chapter we help fill in the gap between the two by focusing on implementation, or how you move from a vision to reality. A useful framework for the implementation phase is to think about mobilizing your safe schools plan as a form of complex change. This model helps us to make sense of the process of change and all the key ingredients required to move a school and all its stakeholders forward. This complex change paradigm was developed in the business world[33] but has been adapted to a wide variety of settings, including schools.[34] The original model identified the importance of vision, skills, incentives, resources and an action plan in effecting change. To this model we have added relationships as another key element. This adapted model, depicted below, identifies the different types of negative results that occur when one of these key ingredients is missing.

Critical Ingredients for Managing Complex Change							Outcome
	Relationships	Skills	Incentives	Resources	Action Plan	=	Confusion
Vision		Skills	Incentives	Resources	Action Plan	=	Mistrust
Vision	Relationships		Incentives	Resources	Action Plan	=	Anxiety
Vision	Relationships	Skills		Resources	Action Plan	=	Resistance
Vision	Relationships	Skills	Incentives		Action Plan	=	Frustration
Vision	Relationships	Skills	Incentives	Resources		=	False Starts
Vision	Relationships	Skills	Incentives	Resources	Action Plan	=	Change!

---

[33] Ambrose, D. (1987). *Managing Complex Change*. Pittsburgh, PA.: The Enterprise Group, Ltd.

[34] Thousand, J.S., & Villa, R.E. (1995). Managing complex change toward inclusive schooling. In R.E. Villa & J.S. Thousand (Eds.), *Creating an inclusive school* (pp. 51-79). Alexandria, VA: Association for Supervision and Curriculum Development.

As evident in the chart, for meaningful change to take place, one needs not only a vision, but also the relationships, skills, incentives, resources and action plan required to manage a significant movement forward. An absence of vision can lead to confusion if stakeholders don't understand the fundamental value and purpose of a safe school for learning to take place. If examining bullying in a school is considered optional rather than essential, progress will be minimal and individuals waste precious time debating the relevance of the problem as opposed to addressing the underlying issues. Alternatively, a school community can have a clear vision and the requisite relationships, incentives, resources, and action plan, but if educators are missing the specialized skills for identifying and responding to violence or implementing violence prevention programs, the efforts will be anxiety-provoking and ineffective. In other words, you can have a million dollar signing bonus and be highly motivated to play hockey in a brand new arena, but if you don't know how to skate, you will be in a state of panic.

VISION

As an administrator you have developed a vision with some of your most invested partners. The challenge facing you now is to integrate this vision into the broader vision of the school community and to engage all of your partners in the process of reaching a shared vision. The articulation and communication of your vision of a safe school has to fit with your overall school plan and why it will make a positive difference in your school community. The extent to which people understand that safe school efforts do not relegate literacy and numeracy to second place, but rather create a better learning environment, will increase commitment to the vision. At an operational level, your partners have to understand that embracing safe schools does not mean you stop doing the fundamental business of education. For example, integrated lesson plans on media violence that meet curriculum expectations simultaneously address literacy and important safety issues.[35]

---

[35] The Centre for Research and Education on Violence against Women and Children has developed, with the assistance of funding from Ontario Literacy and Numeracy Secretariat, a manual of integrated lessons on media literacy for both elementary and secondary schools which is available from their web site at http://www.crvawc.ca/index.htm. Go to Curriculum on the menu bar.

RELATIONSHIPS

A critical ingredient in managing a change process is the one we most often take for granted: relationships. When a principal sits at a safe school meeting, a successful outcome is dependent on the degree of trust and mutual respect around the table. Partners all come with different priorities, mandates and expectations. Understanding, and even appreciating these differences, provides a solid foundation. A parent who is very committed to safe school initiatives may be operating from a personal crisis perspective based on their own experience or the experience of their children. Understanding the roots of this perspective helps you to harness their energy and re-direct them in a respectful manner toward more diverse issues. A teacher whose union is involved in tense labour negotiations may be unable to fulfill extra assignments during this phase. Senior students who feel they are always being lectured to by the adults in their lives may not actively participate if they feel their participation is merely symbolic rather than an opportunity to be empowered and play an active role. In each of these cases it is the strength of relationships that can make the difference when trying to mobilize an entire school community.

SKILLS

Often when we think of training, we think immediately of specialized training for a particular program. Although program-specific training is crucial, the issue of skills is a much broader one. Every adult and student in the school community requires a common set of skills to recognize, respond, and prevent violence. A starting point for training sessions could be the inclusion of all stakeholders, and a motivational speaker to prepare individuals for the importance of the material they will be learning. The skills required include assessment and intervention strategies. By assessment, we refer to being able to recognize diverse kinds of violence and harassment as well as the underlying conditions that contribute to them. Intervention skills include crisis management, bystander intervention, and providing support to victims of violence and perpetrators who wish to change their behaviour.

Community partners, such as the police or counselling agencies, can share debriefing skills for dealing with both simple and complex incidents. The idea is not to turn teachers and students into therapists, but rather to use basic relationship skills to provide a safer and more welcoming school environment. Awareness of internal (e.g., school social workers and psychologists) and external (e.g., community agencies, hotlines) resources and how to access these are also important skills.

Another important skill is to recognize the limitations of one's abilities to deal with complex situations that require specialized expertise. For example, students who have developed a website to harass another student with regard to sexual orientation or are plotting to harm other students or staff require risk assessment tools and interventions best left in the hands of the police and school high-risk teams. An encouraging development in this field is the offering of pre-service education courses on safe schools, which help prepare future teachers for a range of roles and responsibilities. Although these courses do not replace the need for ongoing professional development in the area of safe schools, they do provide an important foundation.

INCENTIVES

In any system where individuals feel overburdened by multiple competing priorities, particular activities will be pushed to the top of the agenda in part on the basis of incentives. Simply put, safe schools issues must matter to command the attention and resources needed. There are many ways to make something matter in the school system. Maintaining a focus can be ensured in a school system by having safe schools as an integral part of school improvement plans and a regular part of staff meetings. In our study, one principal described how his superintendant required a safe school update at each regularly scheduled meeting. This accountability means that the notion of safe schools must involve more than occasional school assemblies or dedicated weeks and necessitate its integration into the entire school community.

In addition to increasing accountability through regular monitoring, celebrating achievements and success is an effective way to provide incentive for safe school activities. The same strategies used to celebrate athletic successes – assemblies, awards, announcements – can be used to highlight achievements of particular students and adults. In TVDSB, there is a board-wide awards ceremony at the end of each school year where two youth from each of the

27 secondary schools are nominated by their schools for a violence prevention award. The awards ceremony involves dinner for the award winners and their families, a motivational speaker, and an overview of the myriad safe schools initiatives occurring in the community. The students are instilled with a sense of pride in their achievements and contribution to a safe schools movement, while parents have the opportunity to see their children honoured for their leadership roles.

RESOURCES

Safe schools require dedicated resources to move from planning and vision to implementation. First and foremost, there needs to be some dedicated staff time for the responsibility of safe schools, preferably shared by more than one staff. However, beyond that basic requirement, the extent of resources required is often overestimated and potential resources within easy reach may be overlooked. Small amounts of money can go a long way when used as part of an integrated approach. For example, being able to offer childcare or refreshments at an event or being able to pay for a well known motivational speaker may provide much needed momentum with relatively few dollars. Even without funds, every community has speakers available at little or no cost through neighbouring colleges and universities, or community agencies (many of whom have an outreach mandate). Parents are often overlooked as a source of expertise, and many of them are willing to donate their time and talents.

In our study, we were able to provide modest amounts of money to each of the school boards involved and our observations were consistent with this notion that a little goes a long way. In many cases the seed money appeared to "prime the pump" for further initiatives. There is a wide range of community grants and corporate sponsorship programs available and, while preparing proposals takes time and expertise, it is worthwhile to develop these grant-writing skills in-house in order to capitalize on these available programs. Most school districts now have foundations to help support initiatives that may be seen as extending beyond the core responsibilities of the schools. Violence prevention is seen as a unique area for specialized funds from our foundation.

Without a clear action plan, all of the preceding components result in false starts. Once you, as a leader, have developed an action plan with your team, you need to focus on effective communication related to this plan to achieve success. Communication of your safe schools goals and initiatives is extremely important to the success of your implementation. Your safe schools committee may use many avenues to communicate with your educational partners about the work they are doing. Initially, the surveys and audits that you and your committee conducted will raise awareness among your partners about school safety. Once you have entered into the planning and goal-setting stages as described in the previous chapter, you may involve your school partners in the work of setting priorities based on your research findings. This, again, will raise awareness among your school partners. Other ways of communicating safe school action plans include the following:

Communicating Safe School Action Plans

Regular reporting to the School Council by the parent representatives on the safe schools committee.

Regular reporting to student council by the student representatives on the safe schools committee.

Regular reporting to staff by the staff representative on the safe schools committee.

Articles in the newsletter including information about your safe school goals and any programming that you have introduced as a result.

Articles on the web site, along with links to safe school web sites.

Self tests on the web site that students may take to gauge their own awareness of social issues, including bullying, cyber bullying, harassment, drug and alcohol use, and safe sex.

Communication with parents when their child is involved in bullying, either as the victim or the bully. The follow-up procedures to incidents of bullying behaviour are extremely important and need to involve the parents of the children involved.

In the implementation stage you may still face new challenges. Thinking ahead about these challenges can better prepare you for their occurrence. Four common examples that emerged in our study were: 1) frequent turnover among administrators; 2) increases in reporting violence with implementation of new programs; 3) intermittent crises; 4) difficulty developing and sustaining committees with community partners; and, 5) external changes that derail specific goals. In the following section we describe each of these with possible solutions. The point here is not to provide an exhaustive list of implementation challenges and their definitive answers, but to identify a few challenges and show how a change in perspective or anticipation of the problem can make them bumps or detours rather than full out roadblocks. We identify the challenge, then demonstrate the difference between responding to the immediate challenge in an isolated way and responding within the context of your comprehensive approach.

CHALLENGE #1: FREQUENT TURNOVER AMONG ADMINISTRATORS

Problem: Administrators rarely stay at the same school beyond a few years. At some schools the frequent turnover of principals and vice-principals hampers long-term planning and sustainable progress.

Isolated response: Each time an administrator starts at a new school they feel a need to establish new priorities and may overlook the important initiatives already underway in the school.

Responding as part of a comprehensive approach:

Although administrators want to put their imprint on their new assignment, the key is to find a balance between continuity and innovation. Abandoning everything a school has already developed causes an unnecessary setback in progress and is also demoralizing for the staff involved. With administrative turnover, staff may feel that they do not need to implement new initiatives because these will evaporate with the next administrative change. Creating continuity sends an important message about the importance of safe schools and a school's reputation in this regard. By using the Principal's Checklist described in Chapter 4 in this book, administrators will be able to identify the strengths and weaknesses of their new schools. From this assessment, they can enhance existing initiatives and address remaining challenges and gaps.

CHALLENGE #2: INCREASES IN REPORTING OF VIOLENCE WITH IMPLEMENTATION OF NEW PROGRAMS

Problem: Some schools may experience an increase in reports of incidents of bullying behaviour and of violent acts when a new bullying prevention program is introduced. To staff and students it may appear that your efforts have made things worse since there is an increase of violence in your school.

Isolated response: The action plan is not working. Abandon it and choose a different program or go back to the drawing board.

Responding as part of a comprehensive approach:

Although an apparent rise in bullying can feel very discouraging to those who have worked hard to establish goals and implement programs that will make your school a safer place to be, it is entirely consistent with what can be expected in schools where successful violence prevention initiatives are underway. It is important that you communicate this possibility to your staff and students.

There are many reasons for this potential rise in reporting. First, as students' perceptions of the range of behaviours included in bullying grow, there may be more reports (e.g., they now understand that bullying is not just about punching and kicking). Furthermore, once students have a vehicle for reporting bullying through an anonymous reporting system, or they are made more aware of the responsibility of the bystanders to report incidents of bullying, it is only natural that the incidents of reporting increase. In fact, it is a very good sign that your program is working. It is important to communicate to your educational partners that there may be an apparent increase in incidents of violence once your new program starts running. Raising the possibility of this apparent increase early in the planning stages will help people anticipate it and understand it in the appropriate context, rather than being left to draw their own conclusions.

CHALLENGE #3: AN UNPREDICTABLE CRISIS

Problem: Your thoughtful and deliberate approach to planning and implementing a safe school plan can be derailed by a significant crisis such as a suicide attempt or well publicized act of violence in the school. The crisis triggers both internal and external pressure to take immediate corrective action and the conclusion may be drawn that whatever the school is doing is not working. It can be especially demoralizing when the media draws the assumption that the occurrence indicates that the school and administration are completely clueless or apathetic about violence prevention.

Isolated response: You allow the pressure and momentum to push you into an impulsive and drastic response, or discard your direction to date because you buy into the notion that it is not working. Alternatively, the initial response might include elements of denial and defensiveness and the incident is covered up or attributed to individual pathology of the student.

Responding as part of a comprehensive approach:

The first response is to ensure the immediate safety of individuals involved in a critical incident and to create an opportunity for debriefing for all those affected including witnesses. Openness rather than defensiveness allows leaders in the school to examine what transpired and the broader meaning of the event. Every violent incident represents a teachable moment both in regards to prevention and effective response. For example, a local school ended up on the front page of the newspaper because of grade 8 boys bullying a younger female student who was a member of a visible minority group. The initial response was silence for fear that the publicity would harm the school's reputation. After a sober second thought the incident was thoroughly analyzed and interventions were provided for the students on the role of bystander responsibility and behaviour. In addition, the incident highlighted the unique challenge faced by boys who want to confront racist and sexist attitudes. A neighbouring school developed a lesson plan on bullying from this teachable moment and posted the lesson plan for other schools to use through an online sharing mechanism. Thus, the incident triggered an enhancement to what was already in place, but was not used as an excuse to abandon the numerous appropriate violence prevention strategies already underway.

CHALLENGE #4: DIFFICULTY DEVELOPING AND SUSTAINING COMMITTEES WITH COMMUNITY PARTNERS

Problem: The importance of a multi-stakeholder safe schools committee is largely recognized (and in some cases mandated by provincial policy), but it can be very difficult to find parent and community partners willing to be involved with this committee in an ongoing manner.

Isolated response: Interpret the lack of volunteers as evidence that parents and community partners don't have the time or interest to be involved.

Responding as part of a comprehensive approach:

Knowing at the outset that the challenge of mobilizing a committee is a common one helps administrators reframe their role to one of engagement instead of merely invitation. Understanding the unique barriers faced by parents in your school community will help you develop specific strategies. Parents and community partners are motivated by opportunities to make a difference when they feel welcomed and they sense that their input is valued.

In schools where there is an active safe schools committee, principals report that they cannot imagine how they could manage their safe schools agenda without the contribution of the committee. Strategies that seemed to make a difference include starting small with one or two members from each educational partner and finding convenient times as well as providing food and childcare. It is important to develop a plan that can be operationalized so that the committee can experience successes in terms of seeing goals realized. Without the specificity provided by timelines and articulated goals, the committee can find itself meeting without purpose and rehashing the same ground.

Problem: Every government and school board identifies new emerging priorities for the education system. At the school level, it may feel like educators have to hit a moving and ever-changing target that distracts them from their current planning process.

Isolated response: You allow yourself to be swept up by new initiatives and drop excellent programs for which significant expenditures in terms of time, energy, and other resources were invested.

Responding as part of a comprehensive approach:

The reality of education is that everyone has ideas on how to make it better and government and school board leaders want to leave a legacy in reforming the education system. At the school level, educators have to find ways to reframe new directions to align with their own existing priorities. Each new directive requires careful evaluation to determine whether it does indeed represent a truly new requirement that should be addressed, or whether it is another facet of an initiative already underway. We would not minimize the importance of a new directive that addresses a previously ignored problem, such as the increasing recognition that sexual harassment is a pervasive problem in our schools that needs to be addressed explicitly and not solely under the umbrella of a larger anti-bullying strategy. Schools have to engage in a critical examination of their programs and policies to ensure that they are up-to-date. For example, a code of conduct that does not include policies and procedures pertaining to cyber bullying is woefully inadequate. At the same time, other centrally announced changes are more superficial than substantive. For example, we have seen emphasis shift between anti-bullying initiatives, healthy relationships, and character education during the past 10 years. The reality is that these frameworks are more similar than not and shifting from an anti-bullying framework to one of character education does not require discarding the good initiatives underway in your school.

SUMMARY

This chapter highlights the requisite components and significant challenges in implementing comprehensive safe school plans. Making a vision come to life requires relationships, skills, incentives, resources and an action plan. Missing even one of these ingredients can potentially derail all the other good work being done. We have identified some of the common challenges faced in this process and demonstrated how principals need to move from a reactive response that approaches these challenges in isolation to responding as part of a comprehensive approach. Engaging stakeholders to be active partners in the commitment to safe schools allows educators to weather crises and changing external pressures. In our final chapter, we examine the ultimate challenge of sustainability. Sustainability doesn't mean fending off any threats to status quo, but rather maintaining a commitment to safe schools, through a clear process of critical analysis and continuous improvement.

In the last chapter we addressed the complexities of implementation and showed how overlooking an essential component can derail an otherwise sound plan. If you have successfully implemented your plan – congratulations! – reaching this stage requires energy, planning, coordination, and commitment. Make sure you take the time to celebrate your success.

The challenge now, is to shift from making it happen to keeping it happening. This sustainability can be more challenging than it sounds, because it is more than doing the same thing over and over. It requires finding a balance between continuing to implement things that are working, but also continuing to reassess and refine your strategies. It requires responding to new challenges in a thoughtful and systematic way such that you do not discard your other successes.

First and foremost, sustainability is built on the strong foundation of thoughtful assessment, strategy selection and implementation that has been outlined throughout this book. When you have built a system of response rather than grabbing piecemeal initiatives, you have developed the capacity for the ongoing improvement and renewal that characterize sustainability. In this chapter, we briefly review the major ideas presented in this book that taken together provide this necessary foundation. We examine these ideas in the context of our research and collaboration with schools.

SAFE SCHOOLS WILL REMAIN A PRIORITY FOR STUDENTS, PARENTS AND EDUCATORS

When my superintendent comes in for a visit there's an item on the sheet that he brings in with him in terms of our progress with safe schools. And it's an expectation that during each school year you will bring a safe school team together and reflect on the initiatives that you had put in place for a school year and to make any amendments or identify maybe a different goal for the next school year. (Principal)

Safe schools are here to stay. Concern about safe schools can no longer only be triggered by a stabbing or shooting in an area school. Safe schools are now considered to be an integral part of a caring learning environment and essential for student learning and well-being. Safe schools have to become part of an overall school improvement plan and not be considered an optional activity. Ideally, when directors of education and superintendents assess the progress and success of their schools, safe schools will be seen as fundamental an issue as math and reading scores.

Ministry and school board support and commitment are crucial to any program's success. In our study, principals emphasized the importance of support from the school board in assisting them to make safe school programs sustainable. They suggested that the school board should make safe school programs a priority, and that they should support these programs by providing personnel to assist with training and recommending appropriate resources.

Although the importance may be clear, there is no simple recipe for safe schools. Educators receive hundreds of brochures each year that explain the problem differently and offer different solutions, ranging from one time initiatives to expensive comprehensive programs. The truth is that while some of these initiatives are better than others, the real challenge lies in determining which of these are most appropriate for *your* school. From our surveys with principals, we know that there is a high level of commitment to address safe school issues, but also a sense of being overwhelmed with options. The vast majority of principals surveyed indicated that they would like a framework to help them select programs that match the unique characteristics of their school and community. As well, they are seeking much clearer understanding at the outset as to the time and resources required to implement various strategies.

As all partners come to recognize safe schools as a priority, it should be easier to get commitment on the pieces needed to put it together: funding, staffing, training and professional development, and resources. Having the ministry and board set the priority gives the program more credibility within the community. Support may also be obtained from other organizations, such as educators' associations, communities, students, parents, teachers, administrators, boards of education, public health, sport and recreation organizations, community coalitions, local business, and municipal governments.

EMBARKING ON A SUCCESSFUL CHANGE PROCESS REQUIRES UNDERSTANDING THE STAGES OF CHANGE AND WHERE YOU FALL ON THE SPECTRUM

Part of understanding your school's needs goes beyond the characteristics of your student body to an understanding of where you are on the change spectrum. Reaching a place of sustainability requires moving through stages of awareness, planning, and implementation. At each stage, different initiatives are needed to maintain progress. The principals in our study were able to identify initiatives that failed because they assumed buy-in that never existed from stakeholders or because the initiative was too intensive for the stage of the school. Most successful safe school initiatives begin with a thorough assessment that helps identify local concerns and strengths in a school community. An assessment provides immediate feedback and a sense of the school's challenges. From this understanding you can develop appropriate goals instead of relying on those superimposed by external experts who do not know your school.

Safe schools are a complex undertaking that involve many factors and many stakeholders. Assessment needs to match this complexity. The best assessments are multi-method (e.g., include surveys, focus groups, plant audits) and multi-informant (e.g., include teachers, parents, students, and community members). Furthermore, stakeholders have more than one opportunity to provide input.

The type of comprehensive assessment process we are advocating takes time to implement, but also time to digest once the information has been collected. Understanding the time requirements at the outset is an important factor for success because it helps prevent a situation in which action will be demanded before the results can be collated and digested. Too often, an external governing body launches an assessment or roundtable process, but expects the results-driven action plan to be in place without adequate time to develop it. In these cases, you end up with parallel assessment and action processes, neither of which informs the other. In contrast, the lengthy assessment process undertaken by the Thames Valley District School Board described in Chapter 1 (page 4) allowed sufficient time for the assessment to meaningfully inform next steps.

MOVING FROM UNDERSTANDING TO ACTION REQUIRES HAVING YOUR PARTNERS AT THE TABLE AND COMMUNICATING EFFECTIVELY

The most successful schools we studied managed to engage all their partners effectively. Furthermore, they prioritized these partnerships, recognizing that recruiting and maintaining partners is an ongoing activity that requires resources and planning. Universally, administrators indicated that engaging parents was a significant challenge. In some schools, clear barriers existed with respect to the number of parents who did not speak English or for whom poverty and childcare created challenges to being involved; nonetheless, some principals were still able to overcome these challenges and have meaningful involvement from parents. At the same time, even in schools without these specific challenges, parent engagement did not happen automatically. Administrators who were most successful in parent engagement showed an appreciation of the unique strengths and challenges of their community and developed specific engagement strategies with these in mind. They did not equate lack of parental involvement as a lack of motivation or interest on the part of parents but looked for creative ways to engage all of their partners.

Good communication is the key to ensuring the ongoing success of any partnership. In general, the initial messages and language of the safe schools initiative come from the top and trickle down. They also come from any external resources that enter the school system to help set up the program. Conflicting messages—for example, promoting a safe environment but allowing students to wear clothing with violent or sexist messages—may be seen as hypocritical by both students and staff. In addition, regularly communicating the messages is helpful; people then see the priority as ongoing and that it still has the commitment of the various parts of the program team.

> .... *violence prevention and the building of healthy relationships needed to be embedded in the school culture. Our school found that creating a sense of belonging can be a powerful tool to move the school forward toward a positive climate. A common language and good communication are essential. (Principal)*

Good communication needs to exist among all levels—board, administrators, staff, students, parents, community members. For example, students need to feel comfortable communicating to staff and administration and not have to worry about being rejected by their peers for doing so. Messages should be clear and succinct, delivering the maximum message in a minimum amount of time. Administrators have a lot of information to give to staff, students, and parents, and need to ensure that everyone hears, sees, and understands the same thing so that everyone is communicating the same message to all students.

YOUR STAFF IS YOUR MOST IMPORTANT RESOURCE

Throughout our consultation process, administrators repeatedly told us that their most important resource was their staff.

> *The staff is conscientiously committed to celebrating positive behaviours and achievement. Administration advocates, supports, and facilitates this celebration. The staff is receptive to the safe schools agenda. They are respectful, professional, good team workers. (Principal)*

Although personal characteristics are an important piece of your staff complement, much can be done to foster leadership abilities and commitment among staff. Addressing these skills and values in professional development is an important way to develop these talents. A strong staff can help offset gaps in particular expertise or the loss of resources. In the following example a principal describes how a small group of dedicated and talented staff were able to compensate for the loss of a guidance teacher.

Success story...Sustainability when losing staff resources

In one school, the absence of a guidance teacher on staff made it difficult to sustain safe schools programs. To continue some of the functions of a guidance counsellor, and to monitor and initiate violence prevention programs and strategies in the school, the principal created a committee of interested staff members. The committee has continued to move the violence prevention agenda forward in the school. The principal would be the first to say that the school needs a guidance teacher or social worker; however, in the meantime, this committee of dedicated staff has served as a useful stopgap measure and has prevented a complete loss of momentum on safe schools issues.

It is critical to celebrate the hard work and achievements of your staff to maintain momentum.

I really believe in the importance of recognizing and celebrating even small successes—just as we celebrate cultural differences and student success, so we must acknowledge and celebrate our safe schools initiatives... this is what provides to us the glimmers of hope...The motivation to sustain our momentum. (Principal)

Sharing program successes, such as stories about individuals or groups involved in safe schools ensures that school safety is not only on the agenda when something goes wrong. Celebrating success helps to keep people motivated.

Succession planning is critical to not lose innovative programming

Another important factor in training and professional development is the engagement in succession planning. When key staff are transferred or move on, existing knowledge and experience must be communicated to new team members. Initial and ongoing training and professional development help create a proactive atmosphere rather than a reactive one.

Teachers need ongoing and comprehensive training to successfully implement safe school programs. Without training and ongoing professional development, motivation and enthusiasm can drop, and the program will suffer. As with student lessons, teacher training can use the same principles as programs, such as providing teachers with adequate information, opportunities to practise, and feedback on their work.

Using a professional learning communities approach can also help ensure the sustainability of safe schools programs. Research supports the nature and importance of a collaborative work culture within schools as necessary for school improvement. A few schools participating in our project use the Professional Learning Communities approach described by Dufour and Eaker in their book, *Professional Learning Communities at Work* (1998). Other schools use school improvement plans to establish a collaborative work culture within their school. Whatever the approach, research findings indicate that plans that allow teachers to work together and collaborate help to build capacity to implement and sustain programs. In the following example, proactive planning helped prevent the loss of an innovative program when a key teacher was promoted.

Success story…Sustainability when losing a champion

The principal explained that this year, his school's head of drama, who had played a leadership role with the school's theatre group, was promoted to a position at the board office. The focus of the theatre group was on plays that dealt with social issues, including drugs, alcohol, bullying and domestic violence. The theatre group presented their plays in the district schools to raise awareness of these social issues. This program has been widely acclaimed, but was very much developed by this key drama person who went to the Board. The principal stated, "When you lose someone like that in school, it is a blow."

However, he went on to say that it was important to have succession planning. The theatre group is something that is owned by a lot of people in the school, not just one or two. In this case, some senior students were very invested in the program and strong leaders. As well, the school had another teacher who had been supportive and knew what was going on. The teacher who left had provided assistance and advice when she could. The principal re-emphasized that in this case, the students had played a major role in sustaining the theatre program. Thus, planning ahead, having co-champions, and enlisting student support all helped to minimize the impact of this loss. Most importantly, the challenge was identified with sufficient time to develop a plan rather than waiting until the start of the next school year when the champion was gone already and the senior students had graduated to begin scrambling to come up with a plan.

Successful implementation requires creating multiple conditions to come together at the same time

Implementation requires vision, relationships, skills, incentives, resources, and an action plan. The absence of any one of these ingredients can undermine all the hard work being done to create a safe school. Implementation is a process not an event, and a gradual implementation process may be more effective. For example, schools could start the planning process with the parents of grade 8 students who will be coming to the school the next year. Then the school could introduce grade 9 students and parents to the program, working slowly and developing a step-by-step implementation process with a careful selection of students. This process could be adapted as students go through the grades. Visiting other schools that have the program successfully in place can also be beneficial.

I think it's important that we make it curriculum-based so that we reach all of our students. For example, make sure that we include it in the curriculum.... that way we reach the courses that all students have to take and this way all students are included. (Teacher)

Another way to help ensure program success is to make sure that the program and ideas are integrated into the school curriculum and culture. Embedding safe schools in the school curriculum ensures that students not involved in extracurricular initiatives are also exposed to the issue.

Though we are aware that there are a number of students who are involved in leadership initiatives such as ESP and Trinity Theatre, it's important to note that not all students are involved in these initiatives. Not all students feel confident enough to go for programs such as this. So whatever we decide to do with regards to safe schools, I think it's important that we make it curriculum-based so that we reach all of our students. For example, make sure that we include it in the curriculum such as in the civics curriculum, and the drama curriculum; that way we reach the courses that all students have to take and this way all students are included. (Principal)

In terms of embedding the programs into the school culture, it is important to recognize that the most effective programs are delivered over several years, with each year being tailored to specific development stages for the students. In addition, positive motivation is a better way to help the students learn, rather than the use of scare tactics. There are various ways to achieve this. For example, schools can implement a particular program such as:

- Forum Theatre – Drama workshop themes can include issues such as sexualities, drug use, and self-esteem and provide students a safe space to explore issues that impact them, and generate positive responses.
- The Fourth R – A comprehensive program that includes a curriculum-based approach to violence prevention and healthy relationship promotion.[36]

---

[36] Information on The Fourth R is available at http://youthrelationships.org/.

- The Write Stuff – using writing to assist students to understand healthy relationships and safe school issues.[37]
- Lesson plans that address important topics in a way that links them to a range of curriculum expectations. For example, a resource was developed to address concerns about media violence through critical literacy skills at every grade level.[38]

Creating youth committees can also help incorporate safe schools into the school culture. In addition, repeating the school pledge every day and ensuring that respect is on every staff meeting agenda will help to create a safe schools culture. Another idea is to devote specific professional development to safe schools at the beginning of each year, or with each change in program team members. Finally, having older students communicate and work with younger students is a highly effective way of increasing the importance of the information about safe schools.

SUMMARY

In this chapter we summarized some of the major themes from the 23 schools we worked with across the province in enhancing their safe school initiatives. We began our journey with the hypothesis that schools seeking to create safe and nurturing environments would benefit from a structured planning process that recognize that change had to proceed through stages from awareness to sustainable action. As we indicated earlier this process requires a shift from making it happen, to keeping it happening. Sustainability doesn't come in a neat package rather it is a commitment to continuing assessments of effective strategies that are tailored to school communities. School communities have their unique qualities and readiness to move forward. Safe schools are everyone's business but strong leadership from school administrators is essential for success. This success should not be taken for granted but celebrated on a regular basis.

We wrote this book to support educators, students and parents in their quest to assess their school's safety needs and develop a plan to address those needs in a sustainable manner. We wanted to focus on the special role of principals who are the mangers and guides for all safe

---

[37] One elementary school principal sponsored a writing contest based on the concept of "The Write Stuff," which is geared towards secondary and university students to encourage students to write about the importance of respect and other violent prevention issues as a way of integrating violence prevention into the English curriculum at the school.

[38] Available under Curriculum on the menu bar at http://www.crvawc.ca/index.htm

schools initiatives. We hoped to move beyond theory and research to provide principals and their teams of stakeholders with practical tools. Together our team represented many years of diverse experiences as teachers, principals, trustees, researchers and psychologists. The framework and tools that emerged from our journey came from our knowledge and the insights gathered from our collaborative research with educators, parents and students in schools across Ontario. We started with the understanding that keeping schools as safe learning environments is no simple task. We continue our journey with an even deeper understanding that safe schools and violence prevention have to be an ongoing and sustainable process.

REFERENCES

Ambrose, D. (1987). *Managing complex change.* Pittsburgh, PA.: The Enterprise Group, Ltd.

Centre for the Study and Prevention of Violence. (2002). *Blueprints for violence prevention.* University of Colorado. Available online at: http://www.colorado.edu/cspv/blueprints/index.html

Chiodo, D., Wolfe, D.A., Crooks, C., Hughes, R., & Jaffe, P. (in press). The impact of sexual harassment victimization by peers on subsequent adolescent victimization and adjustment: A longitudinal study. *Journal of Adolescent Health.*

Craig, W., Pepler, D. (1997). *How peers influence bullying.* Available online at: www.prevnet.ca

Critical media literacy: Resources for JK-Gr.12—Addressing violence in the media. Available online at: http://www.crvawc.ca/CritMedLitCD/index.html

Crooks, C.V., Chiodo, D., & Thomas, T. (2009). *Engaging and empowering Aboriginal youth: A toolkit for service providers.* Victoria, BC: Trafford Press.

Crooks, C.V., Wolfe, D.A., Hughes, R., Jaffe, P.G., & Chiodo, D. (2008). Development, evaluation, and national implementation of a school-based program to reduce violence and related risk behaviours: Lessons from the Fourth R. *Institute for the Prevention of Crime Review 2*, 109-35.

Department of Health and Human Services: US Department of Health. (2001). *Youth violence: A report to the surgeon general (2000).* Available online at: http://www.surgeongeneral.gov/library/youthviolence/

Dufour R., Eaker, R., & Dufour, R. (2005). Closing the Knowing-Doing Gap. In R. Dufour, R. Eaker & R. Dufour (Eds.), *On common ground* (pp. 225-54) Bloomington, IN: National Educational Service.

Fullan, M. (2005) *Leadership and sustainability: System thinkers in action.* Thousand Oaks, CA: Corwin Press; Toronto: Ontario Principal's Council.

Hargreaves, A. & Fink D. (2000). The three dimensions of reform. *Educational Leadership*, April 2000, 30-34.

Jaffe, P. & Hughes, R. (2008). Preventing violence against girls: Challenges and opportunities for educators. *Education Forum*, *38*(2), 19-21. Available online at: http://www.crvawc.ca/documents/Preventing%20violence%20against%20girls%20-

%20Challenges%20and%20opportunities%20for%20educators%20-%20Fall%202008%20-%20Education%20Forum.pdf

James Matsui & Lang Research. (2005). *Bullying in the workplace: A survey of Ontario's elementary and secondary school teachers and educational workers.* For ETFO, OECTA & OSSTF. Available online at http://www.oecta.on.ca/pdfs/bullying_execsum.pdf

O'Brien, M.U. (2006). *Implementing school-wide social and emotional learning (SEL) for student success.* Workshop presentation at the Safe Schools and Healthy Learnings Conference. St. Cloud, MN. Nov. 8, 2006. Available on-line at: www.casel.org

OSSTF/FEESO, Ontario Women's Directorate, Violence Prevention Secretariat and Ministry of Education and Training. (1995). *The joke's over: Student to student sexual harassment in secondary schools.* Available online at: http://www.osstf.on.ca/Default.aspx?DN=4891,4263,1091,365,Documents

Owens, B. (2001). *The report of Governor Bill Owens' Columbine review commission.* Available online at: http://www.state.co.us/columbine/Columbine_20Report_WEB.pdf

Pepler, D. & Criag, W. (2000). *Making a difference in bullying.* Available online at: http://www.arts.yorku.ca/lamarsh/pdf/Making_a_Difference_in_Bullying.pdf

Prochaska, J.O. & DiClemente, C.C. (1982). Transtheoretical therapy: Toward a more integrative model of change. *Psychotherapy: Theory, Research & Practice 19,* 276-88.

RESOLVE. *School-based violence prevention programs, A resource manual.* Available online at: http://www.ucalgary.ca/resolve/violenceprevention/English/index.htm

Robins, S.L. (2000). *Protecting our students: A review to identify and prevent sexual misconduct in Ontario schools.* Toronto: Queen's Printer.

Safe Schools Action Team. (2005). *Shaping safer schools: A bullying prevention action plan.* Available online at: http://www.edu.gov.on.ca/eng/healthysafeschools/actionTeam/shaping.pdf

Safe Schools Action Team. (2006). *Safe schools policy and practice: An agenda for action.* Available online at: http://www.edu.gov.on.ca/eng/ssareview/report0626.pdf

Sudermann, M., Jaffe, P.G. & Hastings, E. (1993). *ASAP: A school-based anti-violence program.* London, ON: London Family Court Clinic. Available online at: http://www.lfcc.on.ca/asap.htm

Sudermann, M., Jaffe, P.G., & Schieck, E. (1996). *Bullying: Information for parents and teachers.* Available online at: http://www.lfcc.on.ca/bully.htm

The Fourth R. *Youth safe schools committee manual.* Available online at: http://youthrelationships.org/curriculum_resources/youth_safe_schools.html

Thousand, J.S., & Villa, R.E. (1995). Managing complex change toward inclusive schooling. In R.E. Villa & J. S. Thousand (Eds.), *Creating an inclusive school* (pp. 51-79). Alexandria, VA. Association for Supervision and Curriculum Development.

Totten, M., Quigley, P., & Morgan, M. (2004). *CPHA safe school study.* Available online at: http://www.ysb.on.ca/english/pdf/LE/Safe%20School%20Study%202004.pdf

Wolfe, D.A., Jaffe, P.G., Crooks, C.V. (2006). *Adolescent risk behaviours: Why teens experiment and strategies to keep them safe.* New Haven, CT: Yale University Press.

Thames Valley District School Board Safe Schools Survey 2006—Elementary Schools
Guidelines for Principals on How to Use Your School's Results

The Safe Schools report presents your school's results along with those for all TVDSB elementary schools combined. These guidelines are designed to assist you in looking at your school's report and using the survey data as a basis for your school's action plan.

General ways to approach the data

1. Look at your school's results in relation to the board.
    - How do your results differ from the overall board results, if at all?
    - What might account for the differences?
    - Put the results in the context of your school—what impact, if any, do the demographic characteristics, the mobility of your student population, the make-up of the student body, and other factors have on the results?
    - Did all the students in the surveyed grades complete the survey or were some missing either due to absence or some other factor?

2. Be cautious in interpreting the results if your school is small. In a small school, relatively few students may have a large impact on the results in percentage terms.

3. Do you have other data from your school to help provide context and perhaps some comparative data? Some schools have done their own School Climate or Safe Schools surveys or have collected more informal data on this topic. There may be data from those surveys which may provide some comparative data.

4. Consider whether the results are consistent with what you expected. Are there any surprises?

5. Review the survey results and the questions posed in the results template. Identify implications from the survey results which should be considered for your school's action plan. In using the survey data for this purpose, consider what initiatives are underway already in your school. Which ones appear to be effective and identify those that have been tried before but found to be ineffective?

6. Most importantly, use the results as a stimulus for discussion and dialogue among all interested individuals and groups rather than as the absolute and definitive definition of your school.

Survey Section and Survey Items	Questions	Answer Based on Results for Your School	Possible Implications for the School
Student Views			
look at responses to items 1, 7 and 8 look at the items on respect	1. Is there general agreement among students that this is a safe school? 2. Is there a difference in student views on safety in school versus in the yard? 3. What differences are evident in student views of respect? 4. Do you have comparable data from other school surveys?		
Personal Safety - Locations			
look at the second section of the survey	1. Are there locations where students do not feel safe (responses 1 or 2 on the scale)? 2. In what locations, if any, do the results suggest that the school needs to improve safety? 3. Distinguish between the need for physical plant changes vs. other.		

Survey Section and Survey Items	Questions	Answer Based on Results for Your School	Possible Implications for the School
Incidents			
Type of Bullying	1. What differences emerge among the four main types of bullying? 2. How do the results vary in terms of the six contexts of bullying?		
Context of Bullying	3. Do the results match expectations based on reports of incidents to staff or on observations in school and in the yard?		
Responding to and Reporting Bullying			
Look at the section on responding to bullying of a friend	1. What responses do students indicate they are likely to use? Are they passive or active responses? 2. How does your school's results compare with the system? Are certain approaches more likely at your school? 3. Do the students need more skills training in dealing with bullying or is it that they are choosing not to use the skills?		
Look at the section on reporting bullying	1. How does your school compare with the system on these items? 2. Is there a difference between items that are personal (e.g., nervous) vs. systems related (e.g., bullying cannot be stopped)? 3. What are the implications for staff to assist students in how to identify and report bullying?		

Survey Section and Survey Items	Questions	Answer Based on Results for Your School	Possible Implications for the School
Dealing with Bullying			
Section identifying strategies to help deal with bullying	1. What do students think would be effective? 2. Has the school tried the strategies that students think would be effective? 3. Does the school use strategies that students do not believe are helpful? 4. What strategies could be used at this school?		
Safe Schools Continuum			
Refer to the full details of the Safe Schools Curriculum	1. Which stage of the continuum best describes your school? Stage 1 - Developing Awareness Stage 2 - Planning and Responding Stage 3 - Educating and Leading		
Overall			
Total survey	1. Based on the overall results, are there any key issues that emerge for this school to address?		

PREVENTION

What is your school's stage of change for Prevention? This page identifies some general activities and programs to help your school move on to the next stage.

Key Question: Are research-based, age-appropriate programs in place at all grade levels?

Stage One – Developing Awareness
You have identified that your school is developing awareness of the need for violence prevention and promoting healthy relationships. The next step is to work with your safe school committee using the process outlined in the video to identify changes that need to be made.

- **Actions -** Some of the activities that you will undertake at this stage include, naming and describing the problem, measuring, assessing, auditing, examining, surveying, reading, investigating.
- **Programs and Activities -** Programs associated with this stage that will help increase awareness and get more of your partners on board include: data gathering activities and providing videos, assemblies, motivational speakers, e.g., one-time events.

Stage Two – Planning and Responding
You have identified that your school is planning and responding to the need for violence prevention and promoting healthy relationships. The next step is to engage in some of the following activities and use the process outlined in the video to ensure prevention programs are introduced into the daily routines of the school.

- **Actions -** Some of the activities that you will undertake at this stage include engaging, developing, implementing, meeting, reinforcing, creating, modifying, training staff, planning, understanding the problem & making the links to gender, race or vulnerabilities, developing action plans, wanting to involve all stakeholders.
- **Programs and Activities -** Some of the programs associated with this stage include bullying prevention, character education, and implementation of other comprehensive age appropriate programs and activities.

Stage Three – Educating and Leading
You have identified that your school is educating and leading in violence prevention and promoting healthy relationships. The majority of your school community is strongly supportive of your safe school and programs are embedded into the daily routines and school curricula.

- **Actions -** Some of the activities that you will engage in at this stage include consolidating, leading, enhancing, mentoring, sharing, evaluating, reviewing, celebrating, recognizing, rewarding, sustaining, taking responsibility for the problem. You are comfortable with all stakeholders at the table. You and your educational partners are willing to share your expertise.
- **Programs and Activities -** Most of the programs associated with this stage are embedded into the curriculum and meet provincial expectations. There is evidence that these programs are bringing about change and this success should be celebrated. Review of your programs is planned and takes place regularly to ensure sustainability.

POLICIES AND PROCEDURES

What is your school's stage of change for Policies and Procedures? This page identifies some general activities and programs to help your school move on to the next stage.

Key Question: Are your policies and procedures up-to-date and consistent with the policies of the Ministry of Education and your local school board?

Stage One – Developing Awareness
You have identified that your school is developing awareness of the need for violence prevention and promoting healthy relationships. The next step is to work with your safe school committee using the process outlined in the video to identify changes that need to be made.

- **Actions** - Some of the activities that you will undertake at this stage include naming and describing the problem, measuring, assessing, auditing, examining, surveying, reading, investigating.
- **Programs and Activities** - Programs associated with this stage that will help increase awareness and get more of your partners on board include: reviewing your emergency procedures, safe school arrival policy and code of conduct, auditing school building/grounds for safety concerns and investigating protocols that allow the reporting of incidents.

Stage Two - Planning and Responding
You have identified that your school is planning and responding to the need for violence prevention and promoting healthy relationships. The next step is to engage in some of the following activities and use the process outlined in the video to ensure intervention strategies are introduced into the daily routines of the school.

- **Actions** - Some of the activities that you will undertake at this stage include engaging, developing, implementing, meeting, reinforcing, creating, modifying, training staff, planning, understanding the problem & making the links to gender, race or vulnerabilities, developing action plans, wanting to involve all stakeholders.
- **Programs and Activities** - Some of the programs associated with this stage include teaching, developing, and communicating your school's emergency procedures to all stakeholders, and training staff to implement policies and procedures consistently.

Stage Three - Educating and Leading
You have identified that your school is educating and leading in violence prevention and promoting healthy relationships. The majority of your school community is strongly supportive of your safe school.

- **Actions** - Some of the activities that you will undertake at this stage include consolidating, leading, enhancing, mentoring, sharing, evaluating, reviewing, celebrating, recognizing, rewarding, sustaining, taking responsibility for the problem. You are comfortable with all stakeholders at the table. You and your educational partners are willing to share your expertise.
- **Programs and Activities** - Most of the programs associated with this stage are embedded into the school's daily routines and meet provincial and board expectations. There is evidence that these programs are bringing about change and this success is celebrated and shared. Reviews of your policies and procedures are planned and take place regularly.

INTERVENTION

What is your school's stage of change for Intervention? This page identifies some general activities and programs to help your school move on to the next stage.

Key Question: *Are comprehensive intervention protocols in place and communicated to all stakeholders?*

Stage One – Developing Awareness
You have identified that your school is developing awareness of the need for violence prevention and promoting healthy relationships. The next step is to work with your safe school committee using the process outlined in the video to identify changes that need to be made.

- **Actions** - Some of the activities that you will undertake at this stage include, naming and describing the problem, measuring, assessing, auditing, examining, surveying, reading, investigating.
- **Programs and Activities** - Programs associated with this stage that will help increase awareness and get more of your partners on board include: investigating ways for all stakeholders to report and appropriately respond to incidents of violence.

Stage Two – Planning and Responding
You have identified that your school is planning and responding to the need for violence prevention and promoting healthy relationships. The next step is to engage in some of the following activities and use the process outlined in the video to ensure intervention strategies are introduced into the daily routines of the school.

- **Actions** - Some of the activities that you will undertake at this stage include engaging, developing, implementing, meeting, reinforcing, creating, modifying, training staff, planning, understanding the problem & making the links to gender, race or vulnerabilities, developing action plans, wanting to involve all stakeholders.
- **Programs and Activities** - Some of the programs associated with this stage include teaching appropriate bystander behaviour, peer mediation techniques and training staff to respond to incidents of violence appropriately and with confidence.

Stage Three – Educating and Learning
You have identified that your school is educating and leading in violence prevention and promoting healthy relationships. The majority of your school community is strongly supportive of your school and intervention strategies are embedded into your daily routines.

- **Actions** - Some of the activities that you will undertake at this stage include consolidating, leading, enhancing, mentoring, sharing, evaluating, reviewing, celebrating, recognizing, rewarding, sustaining, taking responsibility for the problem. You are comfortable with all stakeholders at the table. You and your educational partners are willing to share your expertise.
- **Programs and Activities** - Most of the programs associated with this stage are embedded into the school's daily routines. There is evidence that these programs are bringing about change and this success should be celebrated. Intervention strategies are reviewed regularly and updated as necessary.

SCHOOL CLIMATE

What is your school's stage of change for School Culture? This page identifies some general activities and programs to help your school move on to the next stage.

Key Question: Do all of your stakeholders feel welcome and involved in your school and its activities?

Stage One – Developing Awareness
You have identified that your school is developing awareness of the need for violence prevention and promoting healthy relationships. The next step is to work with your safe school committee using the process outlined in the video to identify changes that need to be made.

- **Actions** - Some of the activities that you will undertake at this stage include naming and describing the problem, measuring, assessing, auditing, examining, surveying, reading, investigating.
- **Programs and Activities** - Programs associated with this stage that will help increase awareness and get more of your partners on board include: determining how to involve your education partners in school activities and safe school programs.

Stage Two – Planning and Responding
You have identified that your school is planning and responding to the need for violence prevention and promoting healthy relationships. The next step is to engage in some of the following activities and use the process outlined in the video to ensure that programs that encourage staff, student and parental ownership of school issues are a part of the daily routines of the school.

- **Actions** - Some of the activities that you will undertake at this stage include engaging, developing, implementing, meeting, reinforcing, creating, modifying, training staff, planning, understanding the problem & making the links to gender, race or vulnerabilities, developing actions plans, wanting to involve all stakeholders.
- **Programs and Activities** - Some of the programs associated with this stage include holding regular pep rallies and clean-up days and establishing student clubs that promote equity, social justice and respect.

Stage Three – Educating and Leading
You have identified that your school is educating and leading in violence prevention and promoting healthy relationships. The majority of your school community is strongly supportive of your safe school.

- **Actions** - Some of the activities that you will undertake at this stage include consolidating, leading, enhancing, mentoring, sharing, evaluating, reviewing, celebrating, recognizing, rewarding, sustaining, taking responsibility for the problem. You are comfortable with all stakeholders at the table. You and your educational partners are willing to share your expertise.
- **Programs and Activities** - Most of the programs associated with this stage are embedded into the school's routines. There is evidence that these programs are bringing about change and this success should be celebrated. Programs that promote pride in the school are reviewed regularly to ensure continued viability and sustainability.

APPENDIX C: PROVINCIAL ADVISORY TEAM

Doug Acton, *Ontario Principals' Council*

Bob Borden, *Ontario School Boards Association*

Barb Burkett, *Elementary Teachers Federation*

Lori Foote, *Ontario Secondary School Teachers Federation*

Brenda Hopkins, *Thames Valley District School Council*

Cheryl Nicholls-Jones, *Ontario Secondary School Teachers Federation*

Darryl Pinnell, *Ontario Association of Chiefs of Police*

Gerry Treble, *Ontario Ministry of Education and Training*

Cynthia Lemon, *Elementary Teachers' Federation of Ontario*

Graham Pollett, *Association of Local Public Health Agencies*

- http://acsp.cpha.ca/antibullying/english/backinfo/safe_school_study_final.pdf
  Canadian Public Health Association Safe School Study.

- www.arts.yorku.ca/lamarsh/pdf/Making_a_Difference_in_Bullying.pdf
  Making a Difference in Bullying document.

- www.colorado.edu/cspv/blueprints/index.html
  Blue Prints for Violence Prevention document.

- www.cornwallinquiry.ca/en/
  Web address for the Cornwall Public Inquiry.

- www.edu.gov.on.ca/eng/teachers/climate.html
  School Climate Survey by the Ontario Ministry of Education.

- www.lfcc.on.ca/bully.htm
  Bullying Information for Parents and Teachers and links to other resources.

- www.oecta.on.ca/pdfs/bullying_execsum.pdf
  Bullying in the Workplace Executive Summary document.

- www.state.co.us/columbine/Columbine_20Report_WEB.pdf
  Report of Governor Bill Owens' Columbine Review Commission document.

- www.surgeongeneral.gov/library/youthviolence/order.htm
  Youth Violence: A Report of the Surgeon General document.

- www.tvdsb.on.ca/safeschools/
  Webpage and links to the Thames Valley District School Board Safe Schools information and initiatives.

- www.ucalgary.ca/resolve/violenceprevention/English/index.htm
  School-Based Violence Prevention Program resource manual.

- www.casel.org
  Web address for the Collaborative for Academic, Social, and Emotional Learning (CASEL) project.

- www.crvawc.ca
  Web address for the Centre for Research and Education on Violence Against Women and Children. There are many resources and links available on this site addressing bullying and violence perpetration.

- www.lfcc.on.ca
  Web address for the London Family Court Clinic. There are many resources and links available on this site addressing bullying and violence perpetration.

- www.prevnet.ca
  Web address for the Promoting Relationships and Eliminating Violence project.

- www.prochange.com
  Web address for the Pro-Change Behaviour Systems.

- www.tdsb.on.ca
  Web address for the Toronto District School Board.

- www.youthrelationships.org
  Web address for the Centre for Addiction and Mental Health Centre for Prevention Science and the Strategies for Youth Relationships featuring the Fourth R Project. There are many resources and links available on this site addressing bullying and violence perpetration.

CPSIA information can be obtained at www.ICGtesting.com
Printed in the USA
LVOW01s2005260814

400855LV00002B/2/P

9 780920 354704